11/48

$4.00
Sport
11/19

To Jack
from
Dumbo & Mary Ann

HOW TO TALK BASKETBALL

HOW TO TALK BASKETBALL

by Sam Goldaper & Arthur Pincus
Illustrated by Taylor Jones
Foreword by Dave Anderson

Galahad Books · New York

First Galahad Books edition published in 1995.

Galahad Books
A division of Budget Book Service, Inc.
386 Park Avenue South
New York, NY 10016

Galahad Books is a registered trademark of Budget Book Service, Inc.

Published by arrangement with Barricade Books, Inc.

Library of Congress Catalog Card Number: 83-20977

ISBN: 0-88365-920-4

Printed in the United States of America.

CONTENTS

Foreword by Dave Anderson   9

Introduction   11

Profiles: Thirteen Men Who Have Enriched Basketball's Lore

    RED AUERBACH   21
    JULIUS ERVING   25
    MOSES MALONE   29
    KAREEM ABDUL-JABBAR   33
    EDDIE GOTTLIEB   37
    BILL RUSSELL   41
    BOB COUSY   45
    AL MCGUIRE   49
    WALT FRAZIER   53
    MAGIC JOHNSON   57
    DARRYL DAWKINS   61
    PISTOL PETE MARAVICH   65
    JOE LAPCHICK   69

Lexicon, from "air ball" to "zone trap"   73

Nicknames   129

Index   139

For Martha, Brenda, Robert,
and Myrna Goldaper.

For Ellen, Alisa,
and Suzanne Pincus.

FOREWORD

You learn how to read and write a language in school. But you learn how to *talk* a language out of school. Sometimes out of necessity too.

Parents, for example. Almost every day kids come home talking a different language with which parents are often unfamiliar. When the language is basketball, it can be difficult for parents to translate. If the contents of the jargon were to be shaken well, a parent could be exposed to an offspring saying, "Instead of a backdoor, we tried an alley oop, but their aircraft carrier went to the rack and threw an eraser in my face." Or there's the intellectual youngster who, on choosing a college fraternity, might say, "I'm more the Phi Slama Jama type." Although it might be Greek occasionally, basketball is really a romance language.

It's also a beautiful language. Parents should not be concerned if their kids return from a schoolyard, not to be confused with a schoolroom, with some new four-letter words: burn, cool, dish, dunk, flow, help, lane, pick, pill, post, rack, rock, zone. Or even some double four-letter words: high five, hook shot, jump shot, slam dunk. Unlike some other four-letter words, these are extremely nutritional for anyone's vocabulary, especially for that of youngsters who know how to dribble. Or even double-dribble.

Dr. James Naismith, who invented basketball, did not invent this language. Hardly. Nearly a century after he put up a peach basket at each end of a YMCA gym in Springfield, Massachusetts, he probably would need an interpreter to understand what the players and spectators and TV analysts were talking about now. Sam Goldaper and Arthur Pincus didn't invent this language either. Through the years it has evolved in schoolyards, backyards, playgrounds, driveways, gyms, and arenas all over America; all over the world really. But like good collectors of anything, Sam and Arthur have put it on display as never before.

Basketball is like any other language. To talk it properly, you must understand it. And to understand it, read on.

DAVE ANDERSON, Sports Columnist, *New York Times*

INTRODUCTION

There is one word that is part of every basketball game played, whether the game is the National Basketball Association final before 20,000 people in the Spectrum in Philadelphia, whether it is the National Collegiate final before 60,000 in the New Orleans Superdome, or whether it is a 3-man game in the schoolyard.

The word is THUMP.

It is the sound of a basketball hitting the ground—and it doesn't matter if the ground is the wooden floor at Madison Square Garden, the concrete of the schoolyard, the asphalt of the driveway, or the dirt of the backyard.

THUMP.

It sounds a beat, a beat that is purely American. A beat of the streets, of the schoolyards, the fieldhouses on the college campuses, or the arenas of the big cities.

THUMP.

Like its beat, basketball's language is purely American for it is the only major sport that was born and grew up in the United States. Of course there have been stories of Central American Indians playing a game that resembled basketball centuries before the first peach baskets went up on gymnasium walls. No, the Mayans and the Aztecs did not invent basketball.

Basketball spoke its first words in December 1891 in a gymnasium at the International Young Men's Christian Association Training School in Springfield, Massachusetts, (now Springfield College), when a 30-year-old instructor named Dr. James Naismith responded to the need to attract more men to engage in physical exercise during the winter months. Calisthenics apparently held little appeal for the students. Naismith had eighteen students in a secretarial class and the game he created had nine men on a side so that everyone could play. In fact, Naismith believed the game would be best played with even more players. If the size and strength of

11

today's basketball players is considered, along with the size of the court, you realize how lucky we are that not all of Naismith's ideas about the game survived.

Naismith tried to make indoor rugby, soccer, or lacrosse fit the needs of his class, which had wanted no part of the available exercise programs. But rugby's tackling on the hard gym floor made the players cringe; the soccer balls kept breaking windows; and the students used the lacrosse sticks for a little not-so-clean fun.

So necessity, as it so often does, became the mother of Naismith's invention.

An elevated goal, he theorized would make accuracy more important than strength; the ball had to be large enough to be maneuvered without a stick or racquet. Naismith apparently wanted to use boxes for the goals but the janitors had none available so they used peach baskets. And the height of the baskets was the result of some clever scientific calculations, right? Wrong. That was the height of the balcony (at each end of the gymnasium) upon which the baskets were placed.

The game quickly appealed to the class, some of whom liked it so much that on the forthcoming Christmas vacation, they took the game back to their hometowns. It caught on and in January 1892, Dr. Naismith realized basketball needed some rules. He devised thirteen. The rules, as everything in the game itself, have changed drastically in these nine decades. But the framework remains.

And while it is hard to imagine what any of the students in James Naismith's secretarial class would make of the play of Magic Johnson, Moses Malone, Larry Bird, or Julius Erving, those eighteen young men and their teacher began something that today's stars live on.

And when that first basketball—actually an association football or soccer ball—hit the ground it spoke the same language that the game speaks today.

THUMP.

The game developed quickly. In February 1892 the first game was played between teams from different organizations and two Springfield YMCA's played to a 2-2 tie.

Basketball moved on from there. As the game grew so did its language. As with today's game, much of the basketball talk was between players on opposing teams: "I'll show you what I can do, can you do better?" was the point.

There is one story about a favorite trick of Bucky Harris, who made a name for himself as the "Boy Wonder" manager of baseball's old Washington Senators. Harris played some pro basketball during the offseason in the Pennsylvania coal-mining areas. One of Harris's favorite maneuvers was to break downcourt after the opening tap, wait for the pass, and score a basket. He then would turn to the man he was matched against and say, "Okay, I got my basket. Let me see you try and get one."

That helped get his man thinking, but not productively.

And today that kind of challenge is still heard on the court. When one player uses a dazzling move to beat another to the basket he will often turn to the opponent and say, "In your face." That should have the same effect as Harris's statement. It gets the other guy thinking, but not productively.

For the first four decades basketball was a low-scoring affair—low-scoring more for the fact that there was little shooting (and what there was wasn't very accurate) than for outstanding defensive play. The shots that were taken were usually within close range of the basket. A typical game score might have been, 25–23.

That all began to change on December 30, 1936 at Madison Square Garden. Hank Luisetti, playing for Stanford against Long Island University, introduced a new shooting style that was to revolutionize the game.

At a time when everybody was shooting the ball with two hands, Luisetti, with his black hair flopping against his forehead, raced down court and pushed running one-handed shots gently toward the basket. Many of the shots went in. He dribbled the ball, he passed, he rebounded, and did things that few New Yorkers had ever seen. A Wild West shooting style they called it, almost derisively. But the fact was that the style worked and many soon copied it.

Throughout basketball's history there have been players just like Bucky Harris or Hank Luisetti who, through their style of play contributed to the language of the game. The incidents are notable, a frozen moment in time when athletes or coaches do something that creates a lasting memory. The game of basketball is a game of many beauties. When you watch a game it is all there in front of you. There is no mass of bodies crushing together in a territorial struggle as there is in football; the scoring is all done by players with the ball near the basket, unlike baseball where the scoring is often done from the farthest point on the field from where the ball is; and, unlike its winter-sport companion, hockey, there are rarely fluke scores slipping into the goal by accident.

When Ernie Calverley of Rhode Island hurled a beat-the-clock 55-foot shot into the basket in the 1946 National Invitation Tournament, it tied a game and created a phrase—the Hail Mary shot.

Wilt Chamberlain may be the game's greatest all-round performer. When he wanted to be unstoppable, he was unstoppable. There was a night in March 1962 when the Philadelphia Warriors traveled to Hershey, Pennsylvania for a "home" game with the New York Knicks. A huge sign greeted the Warrior players as they arrived by bus.

"Welcome to Chocolate Town" it said. But by the end of that night it should have been changed to "Welcome to Chamberlain Town." For in the tiny Hershey arena Chamberlain put on the greatest offensive show in pro basketball history, scoring 100 points. Chamberlain, who rewrote the NBA record books, made 36 field goals and 28 free throws as the Warriors defeated the Knicks, 169–147. But did Chamberlain stand the basketball world on its collective ear? Did fans hail him as the greatest thing since the peach basket? No. Everybody expected Chamberlain to be able to accomplish such feats because of his 7-foot-1-inch size and his enormous strength. He was always expected to be the best and when he was the best he was expected to be even better.

"Nobody roots for Goliath," was Wilt's reaction.

A lot of the game's language has come from a dusty old arena near the North End of Boston. Fourteen NBA championship banners hang from the rafters atop the Boston Garden. Each was put there by a Boston Celtic team and each evokes sentiment and memories of great basketball moments.

Two men were responsible for most of those championships—Red Auerbach and Bill Russell. Auerbach was the coach for the first nine of those championship seasons—including eight in a row. And Auerbach had his own coachly version of the phrase, "in your face." Red, and only Red, would decide when a game was over. He'd light up a cigar sometime in the fourth period and thereby tell the other team that it no longer had a chance.

When Auerbach retired as coach, he was replaced by Russell, who had been the star of the Celtic championship teams. Russell gave defense and rebounding their good names and strengthened their fitting places in the language.

Russell led the Celtics to two more championships as a player-coach but there came a night in his final season when he realized the game was no longer for him. After exhorting his players and barking orders to them in the huddle, he suddenly burst out laughing. The Russell laugh is a loud cackle of startling dimensions. The players wondered what was going on and finally the player-coach pulled himself together enough to tell the team what was so funny.

"Hey, this is really something," Russell said in his recollection in his book, *Second Wind*. "Here I am a grown man, thirty-five years old, running around semi-nude in front of thousands of people in Baltimore, playing a game and yelling about killing people. How's that?" His teammates didn't understand what he was talking about but that confirmed the superstar's decision to retire, thereby leaving the game—and it's language the poorer.

But when Russell retired he did not take all the excitement with him out of Boston Garden. For in the 1976 playoffs, the Celtics, now coached by Tom Heinsohn, played what many consider basketball's greatest game. It was the fifth game of the championship series between the Celtics and the Phoenix Suns on June 4, 1976. It took 63 minutes of playing time, spread over more than three hours. There were miracle shots, debris-throwing from the crowd, a referee punched by a fan at midcourt, and name-calling between the teams. The Celtics finally beat the Suns, 128–126, in the first championship-round triple overtime in NBA history and then went on to their 13th championship.

While on the subject of overtimes, put yourself in the International Sports Arena in San Diego on February 14, 1975 when it took the San Diego Conquistadors of the American Basketball Association, four overtimes to beat the New York Nets, 176–166.

Afterward, Julius Erving, who had scored 63 points for the Nets during the game's three hours and 10 minutes, sat rubbing his swollen, aching feet.

"I've never seen a game like this before," Erving said, "and I hope I'm never in one like it again." Luckily for Erving, things went a little easier for him in May of 1983 when his Philadelphia 76ers swept the Los Angeles Lakers for his first NBA title.

Erving, known everywhere as Dr. J, had suffered through six NBA seasons after the ABA shut down without winning a title. Most thought him the player of the age, yet there was no title. For all his success, something was missing. "You either take it all," the Doc said the night that his team won it all, "or you don't take anything."

But Erving had help. The 76ers had acquired Moses Malone, who had taken over the mantle of pro basketball's dominant big man from Kareem Abdul-Jabbar, who had taken it over from Wilt Chamberlain, who had taken it over from Bill Russell. Before the playoffs even began in the spring of 1983, before the first THUMP of the playoffs was heard, the 76ers' coach Billy Cunningham turned to his new star and asked, "Mo, how do you think the playoffs will go?"

With a look that must be described as baleful, Malone turned to his coach and said, "Fo', fo' and fo'." Telling Cunningham, the assembled press and the whole world that he expected Philadelphia to sweep to the title in three straight four-game series. Most everybody got the message. The Sixers won the title in, to use Malone's terms, "Fo', five and fo'," losing only one game. "How much closer can you get?" wondered Cunningham.

For all the championships won by the Celtics and for all the greatness of the 1966–67 Philadelphia 76er team (led by Wilt Chamberlain) that set NBA records with 68 victories, it was the New York Knickerbockers of 1969–70 who took a city by storm with their team-style of play and then captured a country with a remarkable exhibition of courage by their captain Willis Reed.

Their style of play fascinated everybody, from the neophyte fan to the most seasoned observer. They moved the ball quickly and with thought; they took good shots; they helped one another on defense. They captured the imagination of the basketball world. Even Joe Lapchick, associated with the game for more than a half a century as one of its great early players and then as a pro and college coach, was smitten.

"The Knicks relate to everybody's basketball," Lapchick would say. "They are the meeting point of the new and the old of the sport. As a basketball oldtimer, I just sit at the games and want to rip out the mooring on my seat at some of the plays they make."

And that season was climaxed by one of the most emotional nights the game had known. With the four-of-seven-game championship series against the Los Angeles Lakers deadlocked at 3–3, Willis Reed limped through the entranceway that led from the dressing room onto the Madison Square Garden court to join his teammates in the warmup. The clock read 7:34 P.M. when 19,500 fans, young and old, gave the man they called "The Captain" a long and loud ovation.

Four days earlier, in the fifth game of the series, Reed had lain on the Garden floor, writhing in pain after he had fallen heavily while driving toward the basket against Chamberlain—Goliath was then with the Lakers. Reed had injured his hip and thigh and that forced him to sit out the rest of that game and the next. It also left a giant question mark about whether he would be available for the deciding game.

The combination of Reed's sheer desire and injections of drugs that dulled the pain, allowed Reed to play 27 minutes and win MVP honors as the Knicks won 113–99. The Knicks needed less than two minutes to establish their superiority. Reed hit on his first two jump shots for the Knicks first points (the only points he would score), and that gave them an advantage they never lost.

Bill Bradley, who has since learned how to talk politics, said that night: "It came at exactly the right moment. We were high when we came out to warm up. We settled down toward the end of the warmup. Then he came out, got that ovation and we were sky high."

Cazzie Russell, who was also on that team, said it a little more succinctly: "It's like getting your left arm sewn back on."

That is the way it is in basketball. Emotion can take you a long way. Whether it's the emotion of victory typified by Willis Reed dragging his gimpy leg onto the court or Red Auerbach lighting his cigar; or whether it's the emotion of defeat that the United States team felt in the disputed Olympic final loss to the Soviet Union in 1972; or whether it's the emotion of joy typified by the Harlem Globetrotters, the clown princes of basketball, who travel the world playing a little ball and making people laugh.

The game focuses on so many emotions because it's all right there in front of you, men running around in their underwear in front of thousands of people; or little boys or girls running around in the backyard. There's little hidden in basketball. It's a simple game. Easy to understand. Easy to love.

"It demands no open spaces or lush backyards or elaborate equipment," Pete Axthelm wrote in his wonderful book, *The City Game.*

"It doesn't even require a specified number of players; a one-on-one confrontation in a playground, can be as memorable as a full scale organized game."

And every time a youngster bounces a basketball, the potential for a new star and story is there.

THUMP.

HOW TO TALK BASKETBALL

RED AUERBACH

In the days when the fiercely competitive world of pro basketball was known for such giants as Bill Russell and Wilt Chamberlain, the most effective performance over the years was turned in by a short, stocky, baldish man, with a fondness for lighting a big cigar before the game was over. Fans and foes of the Boston Celtics recognized him at once as Arnold (Red) Auerbach.

First as the coach of the Boston Celtics, then as their president and general manager, Auerbach's basketball smarts were unchallenged. Everything he has accomplished has proved his know-how—from his 1956 acquisition of Bill Russell, when some said that the former University of San Francisco center would never make it in pro basketball, to his 1978 gamble of drafting Larry Bird.

Auerbach began his coaching career in 1946 with the Washington Capitols. But it was not until he joined the Boston Celtics four years later that his colorful language and antics began to emerge, along with the Celtic Mystique. During his 20 coaching seasons, he amassed 1,037 victories of which 938 and nine NBA championships were with the Boston Celtics.

After his coaching days, Auerbach's influence continued unabated and the Celtics hoisted five more championship flags to the ancient rafters at the Boston Garden.

When the Celtics defeated the Phoenix Suns for their 13th championship in 20 seasons, Auerbach looked back and said, "You aren't born a Celtic. You learn to be one. The learning is there if you want to be one. Look around you. When the Celtics travel, they dress well. If you dress like a champion, you'll be one."

All of which prompted Fred Carter, who played eight seasons in the NBA, then became an assistant coach of the Atlanta Hawks and later the Chicago Bulls, to remark, "The Boston Celtics know how to win, not how to lose. They get fluke wins, sloppy wins, great wins, every kind of wins. That's the mark of a great team."

Many people love victory, but as a coach and executive, Auerbach loved it, respected it, and worked for it. He understood it and comprehended better than most that winning is its own reward. The cheers, the silver cups, the bowed head, and the upraised hand, they all came after the fact. The fact itself, the only fact with Auerbach, is winning.

Auerbach was called a dictator, a tactical genius, referee-baiter, frustrated actor and more, but his most important attribute was the knack of translating his fierce desire for success to his players.

Tom Heinsohn, who played for Auerbach for nine seasons and later coached the Celtics for almost nine seasons, once said, "I'd rather tackle a whole team under the basket alone, than have Red mad at me."

On April 20, 1966, after Boston had defeated the Los Angeles Lakers for the championship and Auerbach had coached his final game, Bill Russell paid him one of his greatest tributes.

"There," Russell said pointing to Auerbach puffing away on his victory cigar, "is the man. This is the team. He puts it together. He makes us win."

There has been little change in Auerbach, now the executive, as he sits in his loge box and closely follows the game. A scowl still crosses his face when the Celtics fail to execute the fast break. He still mumbles under his breath when a player turns the ball over or fails to carry out a defensive assignment. Often when he disagrees with an official's decision, he will jump out of his seat in anger, stand in the aisle, hands on his hips and glare at the offender the way he did when he coached.

Auerbach was a master at tearing his hair, rolling his eyes, stamping his feet, throwing his weight around, and screaming in anguish when decisions went against the Celtics. He also had a few other special gimmicks, such as flicking cigar ashes toward the officials or yelling so piercingly in the direction of the nearest microphone that he drowned out the announcer.

His bench antics were good for pro basketball, especially in the early days when the league was struggling for acceptance. Like a wrestler who manufactures grunts and groans, he knew how to excite crowds and players. His referee-baiting tactics were said to have cost him $17,000 in fines.

His bristling pugnacity, coupled with the Celtics' winning ways won

Auerbach few popularity contests. Any place he was introduced before a game, except the Boston Garden, he was invariably greeted by a chorus of boos.

When Auerbach started coaching, he found that after a game his knuckles were swollen from repeatedly pounding his fists, so he began using a program as a sort of pacifier. It later became as much of a prop as the cigar he would light up when he believed victory was assured.

The cigar-lighting ceremony, which was to become an Auerbach trademark, would enrage the fans.

Known as Red everywhere except on his birth certificate, Auerbach let his winning and cigar do his talking on the basketball courts and in dressing rooms. As a member of the Basketball Hall of Fame in Springfield, Massachusetts, Auerbach's entire history is recorded there, with the exception of one of his favorite expressions, "Show me a good loser, and I'll show you a loser."

JULIUS ERVING

No phase of basketball is more intense than during those moments when it's man against man, foe against foe, scorer versus defender—one-on-one playground style.

On that hot summer afternoon in the late 1960s, about 3,500 spectators gathered at Holcombe Rucker Memorial Playground, an asphalt basketball court, a stone's throw from where the New York Giants once played baseball before their journey to San Francisco. The crowd sat on wooden bleachers, stood in the aisles, and watched from roof tops.

Through the years, many outstanding players had come there to play in the famed Harlem Professional League, better known as the Pro Rucker.

Those were the days when one could see the likes of Wilt Chamberlain, Kareem Abdul-Jabbar (then known as Lew Alcindor), Willis Reed, and Connie Hawkins, perhaps the ultimate playground idol. Holcombe Memorial Playground was both the place for hotshots to star and for pickup basketball games that no coach would dare to teach.

That day too, Hawkins, wearing a huge smile, was to say, "There's a new dude, they call him Doctor Somebody."

Hawkins was alluding to Julius Erving, the man they called Doctor J.

During the warmups and throughout the game, Erving, wearing a black-and-orange shirt, with "Westsiders" scrawled across his chest, leaped high on a fast break, transferred the ball under his left leg before passing it off, and hung on the rim momentarily with both hands.

With his every move, shrieks and the slapping of palms came from the crowd. Even when he tossed in a jump shot, the applause was quick, almost mechanical. But when he dunked the ball or pinned a rebound against the backboard, the fans erupted in admiration.

The Dr. J. nickname was born when he was a youngster and played inside the high-wire fence that housed two basketball courts at Roosevelt Park on Long Island. As Erving grew in stature as a player, a man, and as the favorite of fans everywhere, the Dr. J. legend emerged. It conveyed sophistication, elegance, style, and control. On the other hand, Dr. J. also became synonymous with slam-dunks, floating layups, twisting jump shots, and amazing moves displayed everywhere he played.

An almost daily occurrence in schoolyards and playgrounds throughout the nation is for some youngster to catch a pass and dart for the basket with such unusual quickness that he captures the imagination and attention of nearby onlookers. Suddenly, eyes turn as he drives past the foul circle, accelerates past a gaggle of arms and legs, soars and floats to the basket and, in the final flourish, he reaches above the rim and dunks the ball through the net.

Then begins the ritual of palm slapping, outstretched "high fives" followed by the usual chorus of "Dr. J., Dr. J., My Man."

Since Erving left the University of Massachusetts after his sophomore year to join the Virginia Squires of the now defunct American Basketball Association, youngsters everywhere have tried to mimic the moves of basketball's greatest showman. There may be no more apt nickname in sports than that of Dr. J. It is the ultimate accolade of playground basketball everywhere.

There is excitement to Erving's every move. When he blasts off from behind the foul line for one of his extraordinary dunks, he holds the basketball in one hand and the crowd in the other. It is impossible to be in the same arena and not be swept away on one of his magical trips to the basket.

At a shade under 6-feet-7-inches, with long arms and massive hands, Erving has become sports most singular performer, the featured soloist in a symphony of bodies.

Given a running start, Erving could jump from behind the foul line—15 feet from the basket—and slam-dunk the ball. Leaping he could reach more than 12 feet from the floor. He could dribble like a creative guard, behind his back and between his legs.

"As a pro most of my moves are impulsive and instinctive," Erving would say. "I can do the things I do because I put in the time experimenting with them, developing them, and polishing them. I know what I should do in certain situations, and that's what I do. It's a court awareness, knowing what the situation is and what it calls for."

But nothing Erving did in the parks, playgrounds, and arenas throughout the country, brought him more satisfaction than the night of May 31, 1983 when he earned his first NBA championship ring since joining the Philadelphia 76ers for the 1976–77 season.

With less than three minutes remaining in the fourth game of the championship series against the Los Angeles Lakers, the Julius Erving Show began.

First he stole a cross-court pass from Abdul-Jabbar and drove for a dunk that tied the game, 106–106, with two minutes left. Then after Earvin (Magic) Johnson made one of two free throws for the Lakers, Erving took a fast break pass from Maurice Cheeks—off a Moses Malone rebound—and scored on a 3-point play that put the 76ers ahead, 109–107, with 58 seconds remaining. For a finishing touch, he then hit a jumper from the top of the key that gave his team a 111–108 advantage with 24 seconds left.

Several days earlier, the Dr. J of the playgrounds had become Dr. Julius Erving when Temple University awarded him an honorary doctor of arts degree for his role in "adding an entirely new dimension to his profession" and "transcending the human condition through fine arts."

MOSES MALONE

Moses Malone cut a new path to glory. As the first basketball player to go directly from high school to the pros, he was the first to make a name for himself in the art of offensive rebounding, much the way Bill Russell did in the art of shot blocking.

After the 6-foot-11-inch, 250-pound Bob Lanier had tried to stifle Malone with his grueling strength during the 1983 playoffs, the Milwaukee Buck center, said, "It's difficult for me to understand how he could wind up with the ball so many times, even when he was blocked off from it. Moses seems to have developed a belief that every shot that goes up belongs to him."

Once Malone (who puts on a fixed, menacing scowl and a baleful stare during a game) began to understand how naturally good he was at offensive rebounding, he worked even harder to become more proficient. After carefully studying the way his teammates shoot and the spin and trajectory they employ, and then adapting his moves accordingly, Malone has become even prouder of his rebounding than his scoring.

"Scoring comes through natural ability," the 6-foot-10-inch, 240-pound Philadelphia 76er center, says. "If you want to become a great rebounder, you have to be prepared for hard labor. A lot of guys don't understand that."

There are no tricks about the way Malone moves to what he calls "the rack," (a colloquialism for the rim of the basket).

Once he gets to the basket, after a sort of a controlled lope, Malone, with a series of purposeful darts and dashes, uses his strength to take over and becomes nearly unstoppable.

Curiously, what most attracts attention are his disproportionately small hands.

After the Buffalo Braves had traded Malone to the Houston Rockets in

October of 1976, Tom Nissalke, then the coach, put him through a series of hand-stretching exercises, similar to those employed by a pianist.

Rick Barry, Malone's Rockets' teammate, once said, "If Moses just had normal hands for a man his size, he'd have to be outlawed."

When he was a 19-year-old nationally acclaimed senior at Petersburg High School in Virginia in 1974, college recruiters snuggled up to him like a woman to a soft fur. But Malone never attended Maryland, the college of his choice. Instead, he signed with the Utah Stars of the now defunct American Basketball Association. Two years later, Malone was a veteran of two leagues and five teams. It was not until he came to the Rockets that Malone's talents blossomed into stardom, and recognition followed. In two of his six seasons with the Rockets, he was voted the league's most valuable player. He received the honor for the third time in 1983, his first season with the Philadelphia 76ers.

After Malone had almost single-handedly destroyed the New York Knicks, the Milwaukee Bucks, and the Los Angeles Lakers, on the way to the 76ers' 1983 championship, some sought psychological explanations for the almost inhuman stamina and recuperative powers he displayed.

After the 76ers finished the regular season with a 65–17 record, Malone predicted his team would sweep the title in "fo', fo', and fo'."

Philadelphia delivered an NBA record four-five-four, and Malone's scoring, rebounding, defense, and intimidation were the reasons. In the 76ers' four-game sweep of the Lakers, Malone averaged 25.8 points and 18 rebounds a game.

During the championship celebration, following the dethroning of the Lakers, Dr. Michael Clancy, the 76ers' team physician, called Malone "a freak of nature."

"You've seen him in the locker room," Dr. Clancy said. "Is there anything about his physique that suggests he is different? He can't jump. He doesn't run well. He's got small hands. But he doesn't ever run down. And he doesn't ever quit trying. The rougher it gets, the better he plays. It's like he thrives on the banging and the contact. He plays his best with three people hanging all over him."

Bill Hanzlik of the Denver Nuggets, once observed, "Moses has the highest probability of getting the offensive rebound of anybody in the game. And on the weakside, even when completely boxed out, he's so

strong, he just pushes the guy right under the basket, and has the whole side of the basket to himself."

Elvin Hayes, who played alongside Malone when they were Rocket teammates, was appreciatively awed.

"I've never seen a big man like Moses who can kill you offensively from either inside or outside, who drives to the basket with the quickness that he does and who is such an outstanding rebounder," Hayes, one of basketball's great scorers, said.

If Hayes could not remember the likes of a Malone, Dave DeBusschere, the one-time no-nonsense forward of the Knicks' championship season, did.

Watching on television as Malone muscled his way to the offensive boards past the 7-foot-1⅞-inch Kareem Abdul-Jabbar of the Lakers, DeBusschere, now Knick executive vice president, suddenly uttered the name, "Willis Reed."

"I would have liked to see Willis play against Moses," DeBusschere said. "It would have been one heck of a matchup. Their game is so much alike. Willis matched Moses in strength and in heart and he could score the way Malone does from the inside and outside. Willis might have had a little more mobility."

KAREEM ABDUL-JABBAR

The story goes that towards the end of the 1979–80 season, Sean Connery, the British actor, came to The Forum in Inglewood, California, to watch his first professional basketball game.

The sport may have been alien to the man noted in motion pictures as 007, the super agent, but in a scant two hours Connery learned what others long had known—that Abdul-Jabbar was the premier center then and perhaps for all time.

During his introduction to the Los Angeles Lakers' center, Connery told Abdul-Jabbar, "Sir, you are metaphysically as well as literally head and shoulders above the rest of the gentlemen."

More than two decades have passed since Abdul-Jabbar gained national attention as a schoolboy at Power Memorial Academy in New York City where his teams piled up a 95–6 record, including 71 straight victories. That remarkable feat was followed by three successive NCAA championships and an 88-2 record at UCLA. In 1969, as the Milwaukee Bucks' top draft choice, he began a pro career that was to include, rookie of the year honors, individual scoring titles, and three NBA championships, one with the Bucks and two with the Lakers.

But his most cherished honors came in the decade between 1971 and 1980 when he was named the league's most valuable player a record six times. The fabled Bill Russell had won the award five times and Wilt Chamberlain, four. Moreover, the Professional Basketball Writers' Association, in 1979, chose him as "the player of the decade."

Before he retires, Abdul-Jabbar is expected to become the highest scorer in league history, surpassing the 31,419 points Chamberlain had accumulated.

Asked once if he could single out one of his many great moments, Abdul-Jabbar recalled the 25-foot "sky hook" in the game's closing seconds that enabled the Bucks to beat the Boston Celtics and forced a seventh game in the 1974 championship series.

"It was an incredible shot," Abdul-Jabbar said. "The play was set up to get the ball to Jon McGlocklin, but he was double-teamed. I came up from low on the baseline and just got it. I then took it back to the baseline and shot it. It was on the baseline, but not in the key. I only wish we could have done better in the deciding game."

Abdul-Jabbar does not only beat teams with his scoring, but with things that sometimes fail to show up on the statistic sheet—the slick outlet passes, the deft feeds off the post, and the countless rushed shots he caused by taking one big giant step towards the man with the ball.

At 7-feet-1⅞-inches, the top of Abdul-Jabbar's head is less than three feet from the rim of the basket. He has a standing reach of nine feet, wears 16D basketball shoes and his hands can curl around a basketball as though it were a grapefruit.

Despite the thinking of many, none of these dimensions were chiefly responsible for Abdul-Jabbar becoming basketball's dominant force. It was possible to overlook his height when he moved around the basket, more like a smaller man, throwing head and body fakes at his opponents.

"Look at his hands, the quickness in the way he dribbles," Wayne Embry, the vice president and consultant of the Milwaukee Bucks once said. "You undoubtedly heard people say he wouldn't be playing pro basketball if he were not seven feet tall. They are wrong. He would be playing in this league if he was 5-feet-11-inches."

When the ball came to Abdul-Jabbar, he was all action, 235-pounds of lyrical power and mobility. And when the defense collapses on him, as it almost always did, he brought refinements to his offense. The "sky hook," a looping shot taken with his back to the basket, became his most potent weapon and his trademark.

Pete Newell, who coached Bill Russell at the University of San Francisco and later was the Lakers' general manager and the Golden State Warriors' consultant, once observed, "Kareem's body is as well tapered as any player in the NBA, regardless of size. His leg development is beyond a man his size. Bill Russell and Willis Reed had great upper torso development. Chamberlain probably was the strongest athlete I've ever seen, but none matched Kareem's leg development.

"Kareem does more things to help win games. There has not been an NBA center who could pass or steal the ball the way he does. None was quicker. He moves from the high and low post, from one side of the lane to the other. He brought the ball down when he had to and exerted far more energy than most big men."

Abdul-Jabbar became the ranking genius at the art of playing center. He does not play the position with the expected plodding style of a man of his great size. He was agile, quick, and mobile. Other centers could not stay with him for each lacked at least one of the countless ingredients he possessed.

Paul Westhead, the Shakespearean scholar and one of Abdul-Jabbar's Laker coaches, once said, "He is basketball's equivalent of Rembrandt or Keats or perhaps Nureyev. In another life, Kareem would come back as a poet or artist. His attention never slips or drifts. He sees every detail, no matter how small."

Pro basketball has gone through the George Mikan and the Bill Russell eras. Some day people will be talking about the Abdul-Jabbar era and endlessly argue whether he is the best basketball player ever or even the best center. Sports has always been marked by argument, opinion, and comparison. But few will ever argue about his grace and agility and that Abdul-Jabbar is able to do things more artistically than any big man before him.

EDDIE GOTTLIEB

T he dictionary defines "Mogul" as "an important, powerful or influential person."

Eddie Gottlieb had his own definition for the word.

"A Mogul," he would say, "is the Top Banana."

From the days when pro basketball was a prelude to dances in places like the Broadwood Hotel in Philadelphia and Visitation Hall in Brooklyn, until his death in 1979, Gottlieb was "The Mogul, basketball's Top Banana."

Long before there was a Basketball Association of America, the forerunner to the National Basketball Association, there were teams like the New York Jewels, St. John's Wonder Five, the Original Celtics, Visitation Athletic Club, and the Southern Philadelphia Hebrew Association. The SPHAs became a Saturday night habit in the grand ballroom of the Broadwood Hotel when it cost 65 cents for gentlemen and 35 cents for ladies to watch Chickie Passon scrambling, Stretch Meehan maneuvering under the basket, Cy Kaselman arching in those long two-handers from way out, and you could dance after the game.

Eddie Gottlieb wearing his loud-flowered tie was there sitting on the bench, managing the team and counting the house.

"After the game," Gottlieb would recount, "Gil Fitch would take off his basketball uniform, climb up on the bandstand and lead the band as the dancing began. Many Jewish people wouldn't allow their daughters to attend an ordinary dance, except when the SPHAs played before the dance. A lot of couples who are still happily married met at the SPHAs' games."

Gottlieb, a chubby man, who always had a smile on his heavily lined pale face, was quick-tongued and had a faultless memory. He remembered the players, the scores, the attendance, the gate receipts, and even the weather conditions. For more than 50 years he was basketball's authority on comparison, trivia and fact. It was common to say, "Ask Eddie Gottlieb, ask the Mogul."

He could compare Kareem Abdul-Jabbar's feats at Power Memorial Academy, while he was growing up in New York City as Lew Alcindor, with those of Wilt Chamberlain in his playing days at Overbrook High School in Philadelphia.

When basketball salaries began to rocket and college players were signing contracts worth millions of dollars, Gottlieb recalled when he was the coach of the 1946-47 Philadelphia Warriors and had prolonged negotiations with Joe Fulks. Fulks was the scoring sensation of the league in his first year, averaging 23.2 points a game at a time when one 20-point game by a player was considered remarkable.

"He had the most amazing assortment of shots I've ever seen," said Gottlieb who learned about the slim, 6-foot-5-inch, 190-pound Fulks after he had graduated from Murray State College in Kentucky and was racking up some phenomenal scoring statistics while playing with a Marine team in the Philippines. "He could hit jump shots, either left or righthanded and was a big fan favorite."

"The NBA had set a payroll limit of $50,000 for each team, and Fulks was asking $8,000. That damn hillbilly wouldn't budge a nickle. After long and tedious negotiations, I finally gave in to him."

Gottlieb coached the Warriors until 1955, three years after he had purchased the franchise for $25,000. He sold the Warriors to a San Francisco group in 1962 for $850,000.

In 1964, Gottlieb, a member of the Basketball Hall of Fame in Springfield, Massachusetts, was hired by the NBA as a consultant, where he was on the rules, referees, and scheduling committees.

"Scheduling committee, what the hell, I am the scheduling committee." He was. He cherished the job of having prepared every schedule since the league came into being until the computer replaced him in 1978.

When the schedule was still Gottlieb's private property, papers were neatly stacked away in a small office that he occupied. There were yellow legal pads, graph and loose leaf papers, all with the names of NBA teams, a list of arena availabilities, and date preferences.

"Sometimes my mind would get so bogged down with schedules," Gottlieb said, "that I would get the urge to get up in the middle of the

night and work on it. But it kept my brain going. When you stop using this," he added pointing to his head, "then you really get old and you are in trouble."

BILL RUSSELL

In the early 1940's Angelo Enrico (Hank) Luisetti came out of the Telegraph Hill section of San Francisco to start a basketball revolution with "a crazy shot."

Luisetti's "crazy shot," was a graceful, feathery onehander (with either hand) that enabled him to average 21 points a game at Stanford University. His scoring came during an era when few men reached double figures and when team totals rarely went much above 35. Luisetti's way of shooting put an end to the two-handed set shot, a holdover from the example set by the Original Celtics.

While Luisetti's gift to basketball emphasized scoring points, about 10 years later, William Fenton Russell, then a 6-feet-2-inch skinny youngster, a sophomore at McClymonds Junior High School in Oakland, California, began a career that would later place an emphasis on discouraging the scoring of points.

No one who had ever played the game before Russell had placed greater emphasis on defense than he did. Russell's shot-blocking technique earned him the title of "Mr. Defense."

Rebounding and jumping were always fundamental parts of the game but Russell found a new way to use the volume of space around the basket. With his rebounding ability and his knack for throwing the outlet pass, he created the famed Boston Celtic fast break.

Until Russell came along as the Celtics' top 1956 draft choice, out of the University of San Francisco, which he led to two NCAA championships and 60 straight victories, no one ever blocked shots in the pros or forced rival teams out of their offensive patterns. All the big intimidating centers with a flair for playing defense who came after Russell have been imitators.

"Russ put a new sound into pro basketball—the sound of his footsteps," Red Auerbach, his coach, said. "A guy would be going in all alone for a layup and then suddenly he would hear those footsteps behind him. The shooter figured he had a safe and sure shot because there was nobody in front of him. Then, just as he'd put the ball in the air, this big arm would come sneaking over his shoulder and knock the ball out of bounds.

"After this happened a couple of times, guys on opposing teams began thinking they heard Russ's footsteps even when he wasn't there and they'd blow layups."

Russell not only gave the Celtics some semblance of defense, but he brought them close to invincibility. Before his arrival the Celtics had never won an NBA title. They had led the league in scoring five straight years and won the division playoff each of those seasons, but were always eliminated early in the playoffs.

The 6-foot-10-inch Russell changed that with his intimidating defense. In his 13 seasons as a Celtic, including three as a player-coach, Boston won 11 championships.

"Nobody can write a story about the Celtics," Russell said at his retirement, "and not talk about Red Auerbach. Much of my success as a pro was a result of the way he approached me. A lot of guys said I'd never make it because I couldn't shoot. My first day with Red he told me right out that he didn't care if I never scored a point. He said he had the guys who could score. What he wanted from me was defense and rebounding. Red and I had one thing in common—the burning will to win."

Still vividly remembered is Russell's first pro game against Wilt Chamberlain of the Philadelphia Warriors, on November 7, 1959. What was to become the first of the many battles between the game's greatest offensive and defensive forces, was premiered before a sellout crowd at the Boston Garden. Russell grabbed 35 rebounds and scored 22 points and Chamberlain had 28 rebounds and 30 points. However, Chamberlain took 38 shots from the field and Russell had 19.

Bob Cousy, his teammate, looking back at Russell's career, said, "If you took Russ off the Celtics and put him on almost any other team, he would have made that team a contender. I can't think of anyone else you could say that about."

Russell, a serious, ominous man, but also a laugher, a giggly laugher, was the first black head coach in the NBA, the first black to be selected to the Basketball Hall of Fame, and when he took over the troubled Seattle

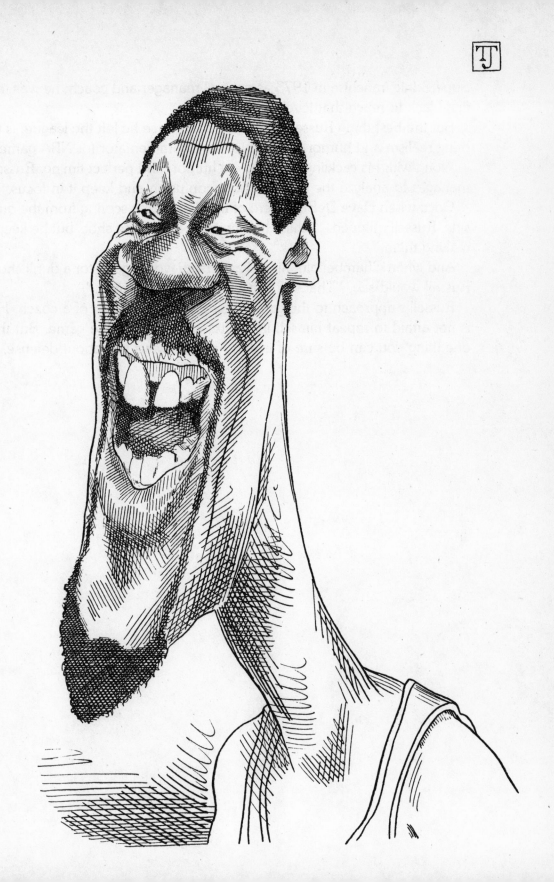

SuperSonic franchise in 1973 as general manager and coach, he was the first black to reach that level in sports.

But the best thing Russell may have done since he left the league, is to bring realism and humor to television as a commentator for NBA games.

Along with his cackling laugh, good humor, and perfect timing, Russell manages to analyze the game without confusion and keep it in focus.

Once when Dave DeBusschere of the Knicks was scoring from the outside, Russell quipped, "I think he's crazy to take those shots but he keeps making them."

And when Chamberlain, his old adversary would go in for a dunk shot, Russell would say, "That's a high percentage shot there."

Russell's approach to the game basically has been that of a coach. He is not afraid to repeat himself in analyzing the drift of the game. But the one thing you can be sure of is that he will always talk about defense.

BOB COUSY

On March 17, 1963, everybody at the Boston Garden was singing, "We Love You Cooz."

It was the fans' tribute to Bob Cousy, who became a Boston Celtic by the luck of the draw and stayed around for 13 seasons to become known as "The Houdini of the Hardwoods" and "The Babe Ruth of Basketball."

As Cousy stood at center court that St. Patrick's Day for his farewell address, he was leaving behind a place in history for himself, and a legacy to every youngster who has ever dribbled a basketball.

Have you ever seen a boy trying to dribble behind his back? When invariably he lost the ball, another would yell out, "Who do you think you are—Cousy?"

Even coaches got caught up in the spirit of using Cousy's name as an example of backcourt excellence. When they wanted to describe one of their talented backcourt prospects, they would invariably say, "Know how good this kid of mine is. He's another Cousy, that's how good he is."

Playmaking is an art and Cousy was its artist. As a player, at Andrew Jackson High School in New York City, at Holy Cross College, and with the Celtics, he handled the ball the way John Scarne would handle a deck of cards. If he was not the greatest, he was right up there. During his pro career, he was the NBA's most valuable player in 1957, played on every All-Star team and was named to ten successive All-League teams. In six of the seasons that he wore the famed Celtic Green, Boston won the championship. But his 16,960 points and 6,959 assists were only numerals; they hardly explained his mystique.

"The playmaker never passes the ball just to get rid of it," Cousy said. "Every pass should be made with a purpose in mind. The purpose being to move the defense in such a way that, speaking generally, the man he passes to is the man who is in position to shoot and, more important still, to take a shot that is a good one for him, percentage-wise."

Although Cousy has always insisted that he never made a behind-the-back-pass unless it was the only way to get the ball to a shooter, youngsters everywhere tried to copy this style.

Dave Anderson, The New York Times sports columnist and a student at Holy Cross with Cousy, remembered the beginnings of the dribble and the behind-the-back-pass in a game against Loyola of Chicago.

"In the final seconds the score was tied," Anderson recalled. "Cousy had the ball near midcourt. He tried to dribble to his right, but was tightly covered. Suddenly, he dribbled behind his back, cut to his left, and banked a lefthanded hook shot—he was right-handed—off the glass backboard for the winning basket. The most startling thing about the play was that Cousy had never before dribbled behind his back."

Cousy has said, "I hadn't thought about doing it. I just did it. It was the only way I could get the shot off." Accident or not it brought him the most fame.

By build, temperment and vision, he was magnificently equipped to dazzle. Although he was 6-feet-2-inches, his arms were disproportionately long, a fact that helped him pass behind his back. His hands were big and powerful, which helped him control the ball.

"Because of his shoulders, wrists, and hands," Red Auerbach, who was his Celtic coach, said, "Cooz could dribble from his front, either side or back without breaking his stride, twisting his body or changing the cadence of his dribble. I had never seen a basketball player who could do that. Everyone else when they dribbled, somehow would tip off their intentions."

Despite the accolades and the success Cousy was to bring the Celtics through the years, Auerbach bypassed Cousy in the 1950 college draft even after he had been an all-American at Holy Cross and renowned throughout the New England area. Instead, Auerbach had selected Charley Share, the rugged Bowling Green All-America center.

From a technical standpoint, Auerbach's reasoning may have been sound since he needed a big center, but from a public relations viewpoint, it was a stunner.

Others bypassed Cousy too and he finally wound up as the first-round draft choice of the Tri-City Hawks, an obscure franchise, which played their home games in Moline and Rock Island, Illinois, and Davenport, Iowa. But Cousy never played for the Hawks, nor the Chicago Stags, to

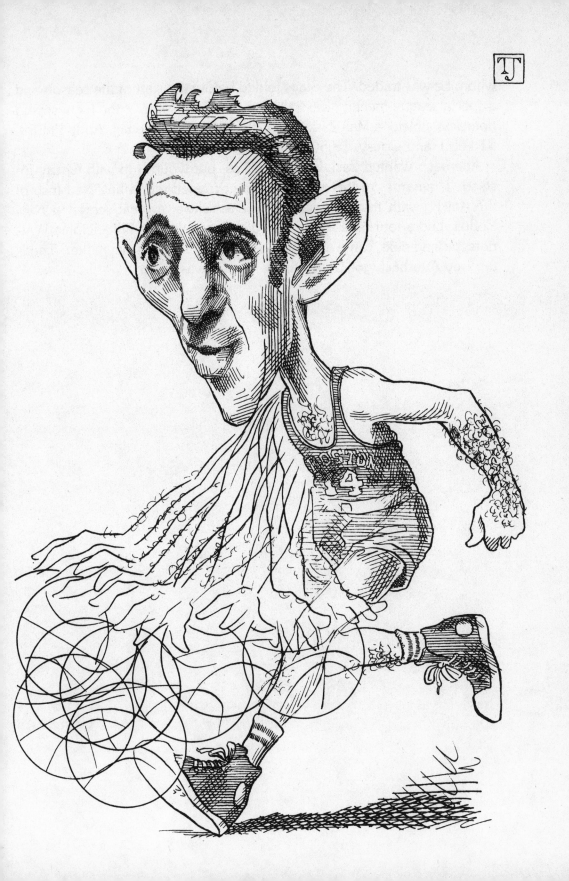

whom he was traded. The Stags folded before the start of the season and a special league meeting was called to distribute some of the highest paid homeless athletes—Max Zaslofsky, with a $15,000 price tag, Andy Phillips, $10,000, and Cousy, $8,500.

Auerbach wanted Zaslofsky or Phillips, but wound up with Cousy instead. The names of three players were dropped into a hat. Ned Irish of the Knicks, with the first pick, drew Zaslofsky's, a great scorer, a New Yorker, and a four-time All-Star. Eddie Gottlieb of the Philadelphia Warriors, picking next, came away with Phillips, a standout playmaker. That's the way Auerbach got Cousy and a legend was born.

AL McGUIRE

Long after Al McGuire's success as a basketball coach is forgotten, his style, temperment, philosophy, and his speech patterns, formed in the streets and playgrounds of New York, and as the son of a saloon keeper, will be remembered.

As a basketball coach, McGuire was an original. Proclaiming his profession as show business, he used the basketball court as a stage. He was part hustler, street philosopher, salesman, promoter, and con man. He was a man of contradictions, alternately brash and gracious, loud and persuasive, obnoxious and charming, abrasive and witty.

McGuire dazzled people with his colorful language and when he left the game it was with a celebrity status that few coaches have ever achieved. Fans loved him as the quintessential Irishman whose temper drove him to splinter chairs, berate referees, sometimes even his own players, and take potshots at NCAA officials.

Although his coaching record never approached those John Wooden or Adolph Rupp compiled at UCLA and Kentucky, respectively, Al McGuire probably has cast a longer shadow on the basketball world than either man. He was a delight to the media. His witty, warm manner, was laced with words and expressions that were known to no dictionary or thesaurus.

Elsewhere in these pages you will learn that an "aircraft carrier" is not only a warship designed with a large deck for the taking off and landing of airplanes, but in Al McGuire's basketball talk it is also "the ultimate big man, the franchise maker." Your basketball education will further be enhanced by the McGuire glossary, "hatchet man—a rough player."

After serving as an assistant coach at Dartmouth, McGuire moved to little Belmont Abby College in North Carolina as a history teacher and the basketball coach.

When someone asked McGuire what he knew about teaching history, his quick wit emerged, and he said, "All I did was stay six pages ahead of the class. And when someone asked me a question I couldn't answer I would tell them, 'it takes too long to explain. See me after class.' We had two doors in each classroom and when the period ended I ran out whichever door the kid wasn't near."

After seven seasons of compiling a 108–64 mark at Belmont Abby, McGuire took his coaching and acting to Marquette where his career blossomed and his witty expressions gained national acclaim.

McGuire spoke on many subjects.

On aggressiveness: "If you haven't broken your nose in basketball, you haven't really played. You've just tokened it."

On his coaching style: "Every coach coaches the way he played. I couldn't shoot, so I coach defense."

On attending college: "I think everyone should go to college and get a degree and then spend six months as a bartender and six months as a cab driver. Then they would really be educated."

On winning: "Winning is only important in war and surgery."

On his type of player: "I can't recruit a kid who has a front lawn. Give me a tenement and a sidewalk."

When he was trying to recruit Ernie Grunfeld, who made All-American at Tennessee: "Look, Ernie, if you want to wear a blazer, go to Tennessee; if you want to play basketball, come to Marquette."

McGuire's vernacular was often laced with realism. When he was once asked whether Jim Chones, his 6-foot-11-inch sophomore center, should leave college early while the talent war was raging between the National and American Basketball Associations, McGuire said, "I have looked in his refrigerator and mine, and mine had meats, pastries, and other goodies. I can't blame a kid if he leaves college when he is offered $250,000 to sign. He can always finish college by attending summer school."

"When I went out to recruit Dean Meminger in Harlem, it was for what he could do for me. There are two sides to the street. There is no way to stop a boy from signing with the pros if he wants to."

McGuire's actions were often as unpredictable on the bench as the words that flowed from his mouth. Once when Marquette was losing to DePaul, he suddenly rushed over to the Blue Demons' bench, kneeled, and pleaded

with Coach Ray Meyers, "Take my car, my home. Take my wife, but please don't steal the game from me."

In his 13 seasons as the Marquette coach, his teams were invited to 11 straight postseason tournaments. But the dramatics often associated with McGuire reached a pinnacle when the Warriors upset North Carolina for the 1977 NCAA championship. Four games into the season McGuire had announced that he would retire.

Seconds before Marquette was to win the title, Al McGuire left the court at the Omni in Atlanta and headed for the dressing room.

While his Warriors celebrated outside, McGuire paced the empty locker room, a towel to his eyes.

"I wanted to be alone," said McGuire, who had begun to sob on the bench. "I'm not afraid to cry."

To the end, McGuire's stunning triumph and tearful goodbye entertained and enthralled.

"Al was innovative, a creator," Meminger, who went on to play for the Knicks after his graduation from Marquette, once said. "Too many people do just one or two things in their life. Al had more to contribute than just coaching."

McGuire's background, environment, and intelligence appears to have prepared him for almost anything.

In recent years he has found fame with his controversial and sensitive remarks as the color commentator for NBC's college basketball telecasts.

Nothing has changed. McGuire is still vintage McGuire.

From the Al McGuire glossary comes such expressions as "nose-bleeder: A guy who can sky, a super rebounder." When he refers to a "keeper", his explanation is, "quality player, good to be around, Bo Derek."

Commenting on his television career, McGuire says, "It's like Liz Taylor passing by in a nightgown—nudging me is Digger, Looie, and Dean. It's just a moment, not a profession. For me there's no training to it. It's like the Christians and the Lions—they just throw you out there. I like having this job, because it doesn't feel like work. It's New Year's Eve wherever we go, everything is sparkling."

WALT FRAZIER

They called Walt Frazier "Clyde", "Mr. Cool", and "The Prince of Madison Square Garden."

With Frazier every move on the basketball court had a meaning. There was beauty, excitement, and a balletic style in the way he played the game and used his body. When he penetrated defenses, sent a pass off to the blind side, hit the open man, made a steal, started the fast break, or knifed through to grab a rebound, he would send New York Knickerbocker fans into a frenzy. He became a legend, the high priest of Madison Square Garden excitement at a time when the Knicks caught the imagination of pro basketball fans everywhere.

He controlled the game using his body to superb ends. He was the leading scorer, the leading defender, and the leader in cool.

Willis Reed, the Knick captain, said it all, "The ball belongs to Frazier, he just lets us play with it."

No guard in the NBA was his equal when it came to stealing the ball. He owned the fastest hands in the East—or in the West. He was so quick that Bill Hosket, his teammate, once said, "Clyde could strip a car while it's going 40 miles an hour."

Except for his flashing eyes, the expression on Frazier's bearded face was austere. He did things quickly and quietly. He was seldom ruffled, rarely worked up a sweat, or disputed an official's call. But when he disliked the way things were going, he would have an "injury" and let things calm down while he lay on the court "recuperating."

Red Auerbach, the president and general manager of the Boston Celtics, looking back at Frazier's career, said, "On the great Knick teams of the early 1970s it was difficult to separate the individual players, Willis Reed, Dave DeBusschere, Bill Bradley, Earl Monroe, Dick Barnett, and Frazier. They were all crucial to the Knick success. But what stood out about Frazier was that no matter how furious the action, or how tense the situation, he was always Mr. Cool, always seeming above the pressure."

Frazier embellished his legend with the same flamboyant style off the court.

A tall, elegant man, he became one of New York heroes during those sixteen delirious months in 1969 and '70 when first the Jets, with Joe Namath, won the Super Bowl, then the Mets won the World Series, and the Knicks overcame steep odds to win their first NBA championship in the history of the franchise. The Knicks faced the Los Angeles Lakers, with Wilt Chamberlain, Jerry West, and Elgin Baylor, in the seventh and decisive game where Frazier displayed all of his talents. He collected 36 points, 19 assists, seven rebounds, and five steals.

After every game, the crowds would gather outside the players' entrance or at the restaurants, bars, and discotheques that he would frequent. They loved his chauffeur-driven, burgundy Rolls Royce, with the license plates WCF and his mod way of dress. Esquire Magazine named him "America's Best-Dressed Jock" and Pageant Magazine selected him as "one of America's ten Sexiest Athletes."

"I guess it's my lifestyle," Frazier would say evenly. "They say I display a coolness on the court. I never show much emotion, And I think people admire something like that about a person."

Few called him Frazier. He became known as Clyde everywhere when he purchased his first big hat at a time when the movie, Bonnie and Clyde, came out. CLYDE was etched in foot-high letters toward the top of one mirrored wall in his luxurious East 57th Street apartment. It was also written on the red and black towels in his bathroom, on the cuffs of all his shirts, and on the diamond bracelet he wore on his right wrist.

Frazier traveled a long road, from the Atlanta schoolyards where he earned nickels and dimes shooting basketballs with the bigger kids, to an annual salary of $400,000. They said he was the symbol of New York, although he had never been to New York before Southern Illinois, ranked as one of the nation's best small college teams, was invited to the 1967 National Invitation Tournament at Madison Square Garden. He quickly conquered. He danced on the court when Southern Illinois won the tournament and he was the most valuable player. As the Knicks' top draft choice, he later danced on the court when the Knicks won the NBA titles in 1970 and 1973.

Before Frazier, 6-feet-4-inches, was drafted, the Knicks were a stumbling, confused franchise, lacking among other things, backcourt leadership. By his third season, with Frazier choreographing the attack, the Knicks, with their helping offense and defense, introduced a new intelligence to pro basketball.

In his career—ten seasons with the Knicks and two plus with the Cleveland Cavaliers—he played 825 regular-season games, scored 15,581 points, had 4,830 rebounds, and 5,040 assists. His career scoring average was 18.9. Eight of his ten Knick seasons ended in the playoffs. Seven times he was an All-Star.

Frazier returned one more time to serve as the high priest of Madison Square Garden excitement on December 15, 1979. Before a capacity crowd of 19,591, his style on court and off was cheered when his uniform (No. 10) was hoisted to the Garden rafters and hangs there with those of Willis Reed (No. 19), Dave Debusschere (No. 22), and Bill Bradley (No. 24).

MAGIC JOHNSON

With his beaming smile, Earvin Johnson, the man they call "Magic" because his game is one of illusions, has brought to basketball a personality as important as his talents.

Magic Johnson is the Magic Man—the Candy Man. He laughs. He smiles. He broods. He mirrors the changing moods of a game. Everything about Magic Johnson, who skipped the last two years at Michigan State to become a Los Angeles Laker, is Box Office. He has taken over Hollywood and all its glitter.

After Johnson was the first pick in the 1979 college draft, he turned up in the Los Angeles area in the middle of the summer to play in a summer-league game. Some 3,000 people came out to watch him and he put on a show. After the game, Johnson invited the crowd to the Los Angeles Forum in the Fall for the real thing. He promised things would be interesting, and they were.

In his first pro game, the Lakers beat the San Diego Clippers, 103–102, on a last second "skyhook" by Kareem Abdul-Jabbar and the widely-published photograph portraying Johnson, who had scored 26 points, hugging a startled but smiling Abdul-Jabbar, set the theme for the new life he was to bring to the franchise.

He became the new kid in town and Magic Johnson shows lit up NBA arenas throughout the nation.

"Magic does so many incredible things on the court," Abdul-Jabbar said, "that he draws you to him and you find yourself wanting to help him keep doing it."

Magic Johnson clearly symbolizes the new guard. Standing 6-feet-8½-inches tall, he was born to be a center or a forward. But no one bothered to tell him. Instead, at an early age he began dribbling the ball between his legs, bouncing the ball behind his back, and learning to hit 20-foot jumpers. So was born the tallest point guard in NBA history and his famous No-look pass.

"I never thought I'd live to see a 6-foot-8½-inch player make it as a point guard in the NBA," said Jerry West, the Laker general manager, who scored 25,192 points during a 14-season pro career. "Before Magic's career is over, doing his thing, he will revolutionize the game."

Johnson's "thing" is passing. He has all the tricks that carve up defenses.

On a given night, while looking right, he might suddenly whip one of his Houdini-like passes to the left into the hands of a teammate who would convert it into an easy layup. Another time, while driving to the basket and drawing two defenders, he will float one of his passes to the open man.

After leading Michigan State to the NCAA championship, and while adjusting to his new surroundings in the Laker preseason training camp, Magic Johnson was less than spectacular.

"I just watched my new teammates," said Johnson, "and tried to pay attention to their tendencies. If I'm going to throw a No-look pass, I want to be sure somebody is going to catch it. At the beginning I messed up because I thought somebody would be somewhere they weren't and I hit a lot of guys in the face. But I worked on it until I got it right.

"Now, there are nights we're rolling and the break is going, when I guess it looks like I'm performing magic out there. There are some nights, I think I can do anything."

Bob McAdoo, who has turned many of Johnson's magical passes into points, said, "Magic sees angles a lot of guards don't see. He gives you the ball in the rhythm of your move so you can go right up with it."

Jack McKinney, Johnson's first coach, assessing Magic's talents, said, "Great passers are not in abundance in the NBA. Magic just happens to be a great passer who also puts flair into it. Some guys try to put excitement into a pass but don't deliver it properly. But flair doesn't hurt when you've got a guy passing off the dribble who puts the ball exactly where it's supposed to be. He's just extraordinary passing off the dribble. He's a No-look passer and really amazing on the short pass through traffic."

On February 3, 1980 Johnson became the first rookie to start in an NBA All-Star Game since Elvin Hayes of the San Diego Rockets in 1969. As a rookie, Johnson averaged 18 points, 7.7 rebounds, second best in

NBA history by a guard as well as 7.4 assists a game. But the Magic extravaganza at its peak came in the decisive sixth game of the 1980 NBA championship series against the 76ers in Philadelphia.

With Abdul-Jabbar back home in Los Angeles, nursing an ankle sprain, Magic Johnson started at center and then played power forward, small forward, shooting guard, and point guard. He scored 42 points, grabbed 15 rebounds, had seven assists, three steals, and a blocked shot. After the Lakers won the title and Magic was selected the most valuable player, he sent a message back to Abdul-Jabbar in Los Angeles via television.

"Kareem brought us here," he said. "Without the Big Fella, we wouldn't be here. We won it for him and for ourselves."

Magic cookies, Magic toothpaste, and Magic coloring books took over the Los Angeles area and Dr. Jerry Buss, the Laker owner, signed him to a 25-year contract at $1 million a year—unprecedented in sports.

Another Laker NBA title followed in 1982 and again Johnson was the MVP.

Maybe Jerry West was right when he predicted, "Magic Johnson will revolutionize the game."

DARRYL DAWKINS

To the average basketball player, one slam dunk, however satisfying is much like the next. But the high-leaping Darryl Dawkins has built the dunk shot into an art form, and he has given each new variation a name.

Prominent in Dr. D's dunkography is the Greyhound Bus Dunk, the one where he goes coast-to-coast. There's the Go-Rilla Dunk, where he makes like King Kong swatting at airplanes atop of the Empire State Building. And then there are: The Earthquaker Shaker; The Rim Wrecker; The Turbo Delight; The Sexophonic; The Dino DeLaurentis, which honored the producer of the latest version of King Kong; The Cover Your Head; The In Your Face Disgrace; The Lookout Below; The Spine Chiller Supreme; and more.

"I dunk every chance I get because that is the ultimate expression," Dawkins would say. "You embarrass the guy who's supposed to be guarding you. You jack up your own teammates and you get the crowd going. My goal is to dunk in a game and bring everything down."

The 6-foot-11½-inch, 250-pound Dawkins had an entertainer's instinct, the flair of a Muhammad Ali, ever since he jumped past college in 1975 to become the Philadelphia 76ers' top draft choice and begin his graduate course in the NBA in stuffed shots and muscled rebounds.

After coming out of Maynard Evans High School in Orlando, Florida, Dawkins proceeded to become the Sultan of Interplanetary Funkmanship, the Duke of Intergalactic Dunkmanship, the Darth Vader of the NBA. With his favorite topics, part hip, part jive, part Star Wars Dialogue, he quickly became the writers' delight, especially when the wunderkind of pro basketball began living on his own imaginary planet—the one he called Lovetron.

Stories of his zaniness abounded and were swapped in basketball circles.

There was a time on his 21st birthday when Dawkins invited "Every pretty girl in Philly to a disco, providing of course, they left their boyfriends home.''

Coach Billy Cunningham of the 76ers, recalling the incident, said, ''There were at least 500 women inside and 700 more on line outside.''

Another time Dawkins sat on the bench hooked up to an ultra-sound machine for a sore shoulder, but discarded it because he said, ''it interfered with my interplanetary funkmanship.''

It took Dawkins until his fifth pro season to become a full-time starter. During the 1979–80 season he played some steady defense, averaged 14.7 points a game, shot 52.2 percent from the field, and gained the distinction of becoming the career leader in shattered backboards.

Julius Erving, the 76ers' All-Star forward, once said, ''The extent of Darryl's strength simply awes me.''

And during a game on November 13 against the Kansas City Kings, Dawkins' list of brawn admirers rapidly multiplied. He finally proved that he was ''Master of Disaster'' when his two-handed stuff shot, 38 seconds into the second half, not only sent the ball crashing through the basket, but the entire backboard followed closely in its wake. The near capacity crowd of 9,180 in Kansas City sat in awe looking at the completely shattered backboard, which practically disintegrated at the insistence of Dawkins' overwhelming strength.

Dawkins commemorated the event in a column he wrote in a Philadelphia newspaper.

It read in part, ''From this day on you shall kindly refer to that historic tribute to interplanetary strength as Chocolate Thunder Flying, Robinzine Crying, Teeth Shaking, Glass Breaking, Rump Roasting, Bun Toasting, Wham Bam, Glass Breaker I Am Jam.''

The ''Robinzine Crying'' reference was to Bill Robinzine, the Kansas City forward, who suffered a cut hand while standing under the basket when the backboard shattered.

Twenty-two days later, Dawkins was at it again. This time the incredible physical specimen shattered his second backboard, this one in a game against the San Antonio Spurs at the Spectrum in Philadelphia.

Standing alone under the basket, Dawkins knocked the hoop cleanly off the backstop, leaving a hole nearly 20 inches square in what remained of the backboard. This reign of destruction, which became known as the

"Candy Slam," showered $295 worth of glass onto the court and halted the game for one hour.

"I didn't mean to destroy it," Dawkins said. "It was the power, the Chocolate Thunder. I could feel it surging through my body, fighting to get out. I had no control."

Both destructive episodes were enough for Commissioner Larry O'Brien to issue an edict warning Dawkins of severe consequences should he ever feel another surge of "Chocolate Thunder" again.

But the NBA never gave Dawkins a chance to exhibit that power again. The collapsible rim was born.

Dawkins was also a major factor in the banning of the wearing of jewelry during games. The man child of the 1970s, an irrepressible blend of frivolity and fervor, wore a display of ornaments that included a gold earring in one ear and gold chains with letters spelling out SIR SLAM and DR. DUNK, his favorite nicknames for himself.

"I got at least two things done because of me," Dawkins says proudly. "The collapsible rims and the neck chains—nobody in the NBA can wear them because of me."

Despite his left hand, right hand, backhand, and two handed dunks, his savaging the ball, searing the nets and psyching the crowds, Dawkins never had the proper training for professional basketball. He came to Philadelphia woefully lacking in fundamentals. Jack McMahon, the 76ers' assistant coach, tried giving him several crash courses, but it never seemed to work. After seven seasons of waiting for the second coming of Wilt Chamberlain, which Dawkins was to have been, the 76ers finally gave up. Dawkins was traded to the New Jersey Nets at the start of the 1982–83 season where his showmanship, though subdued, continued.

The 76ers "settled" for Moses Malone, who also bypassed college for the pros.

PISTOL PETE MARAVICH

Everything about Maravich was show business. He was easy to tell apart from most players, not only because the name on the back of his shirt was PISTOL not MARAVICH. He had long, brown, floppy hair and long, floppy socks that always looked like they needed a washing. He shot the ball from every part of the court, even when he should have passed it. When he did pass, it was not that plain safe, textbook stuff, but behind the back and through the legs or any other way he might invent. In short, it was always show time when Maravich passed or dribbled the ball. When he went into his dribbling act, skipping up and down the court, dribbling between his legs, the crowds roared. Sometimes he would give them the old slam the ball to the floor between your legs and catch it behind your back routine.

Pistol Pete's show was a long one in the making. He came out of basketball stock. His father, Press, played in the NBA and later became a college coach. He was his son's coach at Louisiana State when Pete compiled his three-season career scoring record of 3,667 points that broke the mark Oscar Robertson had established ten years earlier.

Pistol Pete was dribbling a basketball when he was three years old and by the time he was eight he could spin the ball on one finger. Growing up in Clemson, South Carolina, he often took a basketball with him to the movies, sat in an aisle seat and dribbled during the film.

"It was just a little movie house," Pistol Pete would explain. "Sometimes there might be only three people in it. The carpet in the aisle muffled the sound. It didn't bother nobody."

With the eyes of a lynx and the grace of a panther, Pistol Pete began to build his legend in his freshman year.

While the L.S.U. 3–23 varsity team was playing to a pitiful few fans during the 1966–67 season, the 18,000 students, and the Baton Rouge, Louisiana community, including the governor, John McKeithen, were more interested in the Maravich-led 17-1 freshman team. Pistol Pete scored 40 or more points in 12 of the 18 games.

Maravich began his varsity career with a 48-point scoring performance against Mississippi State. By the time he completed his senior year, Maravich probably was the first college basketball player to have his feats recorded in books, magazines, and on phonograph records. For $1 each, one could purchase "The Ballad of Pete Maravich" or "The Story of Pistol Pete and His Pop." In addition, there was a 40-page magazine called "Maravich" that sold for $1 and a book, "Pistol Pete" that sold for $1.95.

On March 26, 1970, Maravich chose the Atlanta Hawks over the Carolina Cougars of the American Basketball Association. He had been the top draft choice of both teams, but accepted the Hawks' 5-year offer for a reported $2-million.

The press conference to announce the signing turned into a circus at the Marriot Hotel in downtown Atlanta. Men and women, girls in miniskirts, small kids and little old ladies, came to get a glimpse of Maravich.

"Pete couldn't get off a plane or take a shower without a bunch of reporters taking notes," recalled Richie Guerin, then the Hawk coach. "The worst thing was the dressing room scene after a game. One of our guys would have a hot night and Pete might score 12 or 14 points. But the minute the locker room doors opened, the reporters would flock around Pete's locker. Later, they'd ask the guy who had the hot hand, 'How's Maravich fitting in?' They rarely mentioned the guy's hot night, so you know how he felt."

But Maravich was not the ordinary player. His rookie season coincided with the ABC Network deal to televise NBA games. Two of the first three televised games shown involved the Hawks and included Maravich's pro debut in which he played 22 minute and scored 7 points in Atlanta's 107–98 loss to the Milwaukee Bucks.

Roone Arledge, president of ABC Sports, explaining the sudden interest in the Hawks, said, "Pistol Pete is the reason. Because of his show biz style and his college record, his development is of much more national interest than that of the average rookie."

Maravich averaged 23.2, 19.3, 26.1, and 27.7 points a game in each of the four seasons before the Hawks gave up on him and traded him to the New Orleans Jazz. He played five plus seasons with the Jazz in New

Orleans and Utah, and he completed his 10-season pro career with the Boston Celtics in the later half of the 1979–80 season. He had a 24.2 career scoring average that included the 1977–78 scoring championship (31.1 points).

During his career Maravich had almost everything, except a championship ring, something that he craved.

Lou Hudson, the high-scoring Atlanta Hawk guard, who played four seasons with Maravich, once said of Pistol Pete, "This man was quicker and faster than Jerry West or Oscar Robertson. He got the ball up the floor better. He shot as well. Raw talentwise, he was the greatest who ever played."

JOE LAPCHICK

From his vantage point of more than 50 years of basketball, Joe Bohomiel Lapchick, born to a Czechoslovak immigrant family in Yonkers, New York, saw it all. The years of changes were kaleidoscopic—the birth, the struggles, the growth, ultimate recognition, followed by the acceptance and the success of the one truly American sport, basketball.

The Lapchick years began in the dance hall days of basketball when he was a gangly youngster. By the time he retired as St. John's University basketball coach, 65 years after his birth on April 12, 1900, Lapchick's career could be best summed up in two words—class and style. Lapchick was more than a coach. He was a coach's coach. His was the only team to win the National Invitation Tournament four times and during the nine seasons he coached the New York Knickerbockers, they never missed the NBA playoffs.

It's not merely coincidence that so many of his players became coaches, including eight from the 1954 Knicks, Vince Boryla, Carl Braun, Harry Gallatin, Dick McGuire, Al McGuire, Fred Schaus, Jim Baechtold, and Butch van Breda Kolff.

There was hardly a time that Lapchick could recall not being part of the basketball scene. At twelve, already 6-feet-2-inches, he was playing on a number of club teams in a uniform his mother had hand sewn.

One day, Lapchick's father, on his way home from work, spotted the skimpy uniform hanging out to dry on the clothes line.

"What is that?" his father asked.

"That's my basketball uniform, Dad," the young man replied.

"You mean you appear in front of people dressed like that?" shouted the father.

After his graduation from grammar school, Lapchick worked as a golf caddy and later in a factory, working a 10-hour day for about $15 a week. But he soon found it more profitable to hang around the information booth at Grand Central Terminal juggling offers from the Holyoke Reds, the Brooklyn Visitations and other clubs. A good negotiator, he worked his way up to $75 a game.

Finally, Lapchick got to play against the best team in the area, the New York Celtics, and their experienced center, Horse Haggerty. When Haggerty wore out in the early 1920s, Lapchick joined the Celtics, the finest team of that day, not big by today's standards, but rough and tough.

That was Lapchick's beginning of a four-stage career, each marked by success, and each having had an overwhelming influence on the world of basketball.

In his twenties, as a player, he was a "giant" at 6-feet-5-inches, in a day of few 6-footers—skinny and tough. He won most fame as a member of the Original Celtics, the team that dominated the sport so thoroughly in the 1920s that no effective league could be formed around it.

His more famous teammate, Nat Holman, was already coaching at City College and was recognized as the greatest player. But even then, Lapchick began to learn and prove the facts of basketball's future—the overwhelming importance of getting the ball, and therefore, the inescapable supremacy of the big man.

In 1936, with only a grammar school education and no teaching experience, he became the St. John's coach during a time when college basketball grew from a sport played before a handful of people in school gymnasiums, to the capacity crowds of more than 18,000 in Madison Square Garden.

When he became the coach of the Knicks in 1947, he did for the fledgling NBA what he did at St. John's and for college basketball—in educating the press and the public in basketball's inner dramas, Lapchick was of supreme importance.

But pro basketball, with its then 70-game schedule and one-night stands made a wreck out of Lapchick. Sometimes he would rip off his jacket, pull the sleeves inside out and stomp on it. Another time he threw the water tray in the air and it fell on his head.

Finally, in 1956, at the age of 56, he returned as the St. John's coach at a time when recruiting competition for players was far more extensive than any he had faced. Under his coaching, the Big Indian, as he was affectionately known, helped both the Redmen and the college game grow in stature.

During the 1964–65 season, his players, realizing Lapchick was being forced into retirement at the mandatory age of 65, dedicated themselves to "winning for the coach." St. John's beat highly-favored Michigan in the Holiday Festival in December of 1964 and several months later sent Lapchick into retirement with a 55–51 victory over Villanova in the final of the National Invitation Tournament.

As his players hoisted him on to their shoulders and carried him off the Garden floor, Lapchick shouted, "What a way to go."

Pride was the mainspring of Lapchick's character and philosophy. That he had a philosophy, in the most unpretentious way, was the aspect of his personality that made the most lasting impression on the thousands of people who had direct dealings with him through the half-century he lived in the sports limelight.

His philosophy was often expressed in one sentence, "Anyone can walk with kings if he walks straight."

Lapchick died in 1970, leaving behind his legacy that the chief goal in life was lending a helping hand to others. As a player and coach he achieved legendary success, but he is best remembered as basketball's ambassador of good will.

LEXICON

Air ball

n: the ultimate disgrace, a shot that hits nothing, not the rim, not the net, not the backboard, not a defender's hand. The only thing worse than an air ball on a field~goal attempt is an air ball on a free throw.

Kareem Abdul~Jabbar.

aircraft carrier

n: a big man, a center who is a franchise maker; bring in a guy like this and the battle can be won. Kareem Abdul~Jabbar has been an aircraft carrier in three ports: Los Angeles, with UCLA; Milwaukee, with the Bucks; and Los Angeles again, with the Lakers.

alley oop

n: one of the game's most excit~ing plays. A player heads for the basket, usually from the side of the court away from the ball. Spotting his movement, a teammate

(alley oop cont'd)

76 tosses the ball in the vicinity of the rim and the first player, coming toward the basket, leaps, grabs the ball before it hits the rim or backboard and stuffs it through the basket. This play became popular with the North Carolina State national championship team of 1974. Monte Towe, the 5~foot~6~inch guard, was the passer and the astonishing David Thompson was the alley ooper. The pair worked the play so effectively that when Thompson was pro basketball's top draft choice and joined Denver in the American Basketball Association, the Nuggets also signed Towe despite his size.

David Thompson

Monte Towe

assist

vt: to make the pass that results in a basket.
n: the pass that results in a basket.

Backcourt

n: the guards, the players who are responsible for bringing the ball up the court to set up teammates for shots. Also, the area behind the center line when a team is in the offensive end of the court.

Bill Bradley

Dave DeBusschere

backdoor

n: a play where an offensive player away from the ball moves up, takes a pass, and sneaks behind the defenders for an easy basket, as in sneaking into the house through the backdoor when no one is looking. Bill Bradley and Dave DeBusschere worked this play most effectively with the New York Knicks in the late 1960s and early 1970s. Bradley's style of play—nonstop movement around the court—put him inside the defense for numerous backdoor plays.

Dave Cowens

bank shot

n: a shot made by shooting the ball against the backboard so that the ball will deflect into the basket.

baseball pass

n: a ball thrown most of the way down-court to a teammate on his way toward the basket. The pass is thrown with a similar motion to that of a catcher in baseball throwing the ball to second base.

baseline

n: each end line of the basketball court.

belly up

vt: to play tight defense, that is, with practically no space between the two opposing players.

boards

n: the flat panels behind each basket.

bonus

n: in pro basketball, the extra free throws awarded to the team fouled, after the opposing team has exceeded its allowed number of fouls in a quarter or, in college basketball, a half.

box out

vt: to turn and face the basket following a shot and with your back, arms, and backside, ensure that the player you are guarding can't get close

Paul Silas

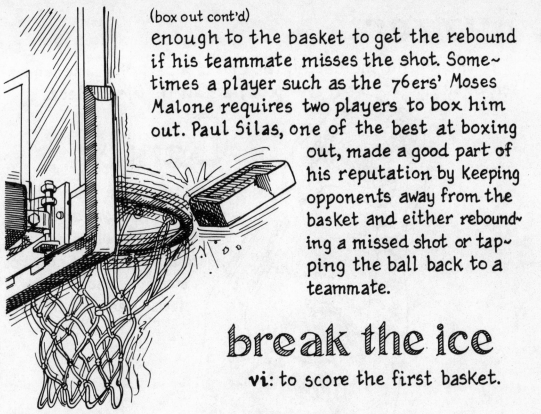

enough to the basket to get the rebound if his teammate misses the shot. Some~ times a player such as the 76ers' Moses Malone requires two players to box him out. Paul Silas, one of the best at boxing out, made a good part of his reputation by keeping opponents away from the basket and either rebound~ ing a missed shot or tap~ ping the ball back to a teammate.

break the ice

vi: to score the first basket.

brick

n: a poor shot made by a player who has no sense of where it is going. Usually such a shot hits the backboard with a thunk or the rim of the basket with a clang. One hopes that a player who shoots bricks is good at boxing out.

bucket

n: one of the scores of terms for basket.

burn

vt: to beat your man to the basket, particularly with a fancy move that results in a score.

buzzer

n: the sound indicating the end of a part of a game (a quarter in the pros; a half in the colleges).

Center

n: usually a team's big man, literally and figuratively; the player who must be able to control rebounding and defense near the basket.

Wilt Chamberlain

charging

adj: a foul committed when the player with the ball runs into an opponent who has clearly established his defensive position (not moving when banged into). If the defender has not established his position, he has committed a blocking foul.

chippie

n: a short shot, one that should never be missed.

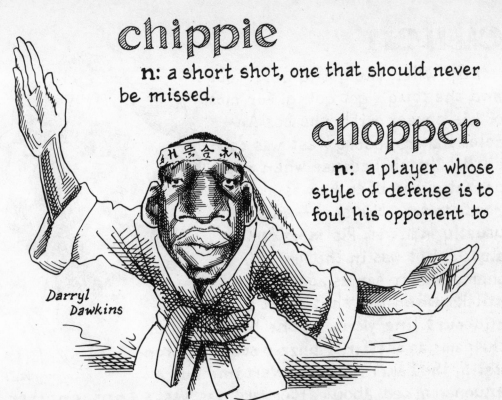

Darryl Dawkins

chopper

n: a player whose style of defense is to foul his opponent to keep him from shooting. Usually these fouls are not simple pushes or slapped hands, but acts bordering on violence that the opponent will be thinking about the next time he is ready to shoot.

chump

n: a bad player, one who can easily be outplayed.

city game

n: the type of basketball played in the schoolyards of the big cities, usually in the East. The term came into vogue with Pete Axthelm's 1970 book, that chronicled the success of the 1969~1970 Knicks along with the lives of some schoolyard heroes who never made it to Madison Square Garden.

clutch

adj: when the going gets tough and the tough get going. For most of his career with the Los An~geles Lakers, Jerry West was call~ed Mr. Clutch because when one basket was needed he was always ready to take the shot—and he usually made it. His most famous clutch shot was in the 1970 NBA championship series against the Knicks when his shot from behind the midcourt line went in the basket, tying the game as the final buzzer sounded. Iron~ically, the Lakers lost in overtime but all anyone talked about afterward was West's shot. Another twist is that today the 3~point field goal rule is in effect and had it been in effect then, West's shot would have won the game as the Lakers were only 2 points behind.

Jerry West

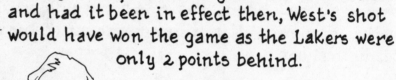

cool

n: the quality of never getting flustered on the basketball court or off it.

Norm Nixon

court smarts

n: a sense of knowing where you are in the game and the ability to know where everyone else is too. Always thinking and being one move ahead of the other guy.

cross~court pass

n: a pass thrown from one side of the offensive zone to the other. A cardinal sin and one of the first things a coach tells a player to avoid. Because the ball is in the air for so long and has to cover so much distance, such a pass is easy to intercept.

curtain time

n: the point in a game when one team has no chance to catch up. There is no miracle big enough to make it happen.

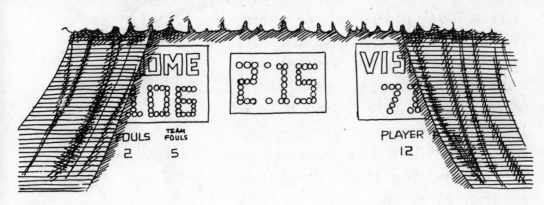

D

n: what you play to try to stop your opponent from scoring. More commonly known as Defense but not commonly referred to as such. Someone who had a good game in shutting down his opponent is said to have played the "good D."

dance

n: the game but always a big game. An early~season college game against a small school is never the dance. An important conference game or a game in the NCAA

(dance cont'd)

84

tournament is The Dance. However, one team's breather may be another team's dance—witness the victory by tiny Chaminade of Hawaii over top-ranked Virginia led by Ralph Sampson in December 1982. For Chaminade, that was indeed The Dance.

dance-hall player

n: a tough player whose game is based on his ability to stop his opponent or to score himself regardless of the pressure by the other team. The term was born in the early days of professional basketball when the game was often the opening attraction before a dance at a community center—a time when the dance was just that and not a big game.

Vern Mikkelsen

deal

vt: to pass the ball around the floor. A team is dealing if all the players keep the ball moving around, while they look for the easiest shot.

dee-fense

n: the call of the fans imploring their team to shut down their opponents. Its origin was probably in Madison Square Garden during the late 1960s when Red Holzman's Knick

(dee-fense cont'd)

teams showed New Yorkers that sometimes it is as much fun to watch your team stop the other team from scoring as it is to see it perform an offensive show. Of course, Red Auerbach's Celtic teams were doing this in Boston for more years with more success but as Bill Russell pointed out in his book, *Second Wind*, "excellence gets noticed" in New York.

dish

vt: to pass the ball off while driving to the basket, a pass that enables a teammate to score an easy two points.

doctor

n: a player who operates while on the court.

double dribble

vt: to continue dribbling after grabbing the ball with both hands. Not only does this look awkward but it's a violation and costs your team possession of the ball. Also called discontinuation, which involves actually holding onto the ball, stopping your movement and then starting again.

double figures

n: the scoring of 10 points in a game;

grabbing 10 or more rebounds; or passing for 10 or more assists.

double pump

vt: to fake a shot twice with downward and upward arm movements before actually taking it.

double team

vt: to send two men to defend against one. The man with the ball is automatically double~teamed in certain defensive formations and at times a team's high scorer is double~teamed in an effort to prevent him from getting his hands on the ball.

downtown

n: an area far from the basket and one that a player really shouldn't shoot from.

Of course when a player can shoot as well as the Seattle SuperSonics' Freddy Brown, he can go downtown all game.

Freddy Brown

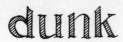

dunk

vt: to put the ball in the basket from a spot above the rim about as easily as someone might dunk a doughnut. Wilt Chamberlain was the first big man to be so adroit at getting close to the basket as to make this shot unstoppable. College and high school basketball outlawed the dunk for nine seasons in an attempt to play down the importance of the really big players. But the ban was rescinded, for it is such a crowd~pleasing play and many shorter players can jump high enough to dunk.

East Cupcake

n: the easiest possible opponent for a team. The school made famous by Al McGuire. According to him, *your* school never plays East Cupcake, because your easy opponents are always tough, scrappy, overlooked clubs. Your opponents, however, always fatten up their records early in the college basketball season with a string of games against East Cupcakes.

Marvin Webster

eraser

n: a player whose specialty is blocking shots. Marvin Webster came out of college with the nickname, the Human Eraser, because of his skill.

Facial

n: something one player gives another when he executes a particularly outstanding move— either on offense or defense.

fadeaway jumper

n: a shot taken by leaving your feet and jumping backwards away from the basket. Often the type of shot used by a player to shoot without danger of having his shot blocked.

fall back

vt: what a player shouts to his team when he takes a shot that he is sure is going in.

Dick Barnett

fast break

n: the quick downcourt movement by a team on of~ fense, usually following a missed shot by the other team. The intent is to get down the floor before the defending team can set up, thereby giving the offense an easy shot at the basket.

filling the lanes

part. phrase: the movement of a team properly execu~ ting a fast break. Each player has a lane, designated by his coach in practice, and if all the lanes are filled properly,

(filling the lanes cont'd)

someone will be open when the fast break reaches its destination near the basket.

Chet Walker

finger roll

n: a shot taken by bringing your hand, palm up, above the rim and letting the ball drop off your finger tips into the basket.

fire the rock

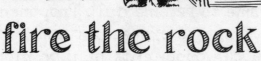

vi: to shoot well, as in "Iceman can fire the rock"— George Gervin talking about his shooting prowess.

flow

n: a team's smooth movement on offense and defense. When Portland had a healthy Bill Walton in 1977, the team's flow brought the Trail Blazers an NBA title.

George Gervin

Bill Walton

foul shot

n: the unhindered try for a point after a player has been fouled by an opponent. Also known as a free throw.

four corners

n: the type of offense popularized by Coach Dean Smith of North Carolina and used when his team is ahead. It sets one man in each of the four corners of the offensive zone with the fifth man designated to handle the ball much of the time. When the defense tries to double team the man with the ball, he is supposed to pass it off to one of the men in the four corners. Critics say that this style of play does two things, both of them bad. First, it takes a team in the lead out of its offensive flow and, second, it causes the game to become dull. Proponents say that it is an effective way to protect a team if it is holding the lead although the opponents may be more talented or if a team has players who are tired or in foul trouble. Styles of play such as this led to the introduction of a shot clock in many college conferences for the 1982~83 season.

free foul

n: anything a player can get away with. If the referee doesn't call you for a foul as you use your free arm to hold off a defensive player

Oscar Robertson

while you are dribbling, you have gotten a free foul. Oscar Robertson spent 14 years in the NBA and was rarely
cited for his free foul, which the players called a "club."

freeze

n: a way of hold-
ing on to the ball to protect a lead.

vt: to hold the ball to
use up the time on the game
clock.

Kevin Porter

French pastry

n: performing unneces-
sarily. Making an easy shot
look tough and a tough shot
look tougher.

fullcourt press

n: the tactic of applying defensive pressure even before
a team moves the ball inbounds and maintaining that
pressure all the way downcourt (also known as an allcourt
press). Usually used by a team that is trailing, but it is
also effective when used by a team with a small lead
that wants to extend the lead while the other team
has weak ball handlers in the game.

Kelly Tripucka

Garbage man

n: a player who only scores on short

shots with no one guarding him.

garbage time

n: the last few minutes of the game, when the outcome has been decided and the last substitutes on the bench are in the game. Their baskets are scored without any pattern, grace, or apparent skill.

get back

vt: to hustle back on defense.

give and go

n: a play designed to catch a defender napping. After you "give" the ball to a teammate, you "go" towards the basket, hoping that your defender has eased up when he saw you pass the ball away. If he has, your teammate gets the ball back to you near the basket for a shot.

Mike Riordan

give one

vt: to commit an inten-tional foul, usually to stop a team's momentum, and in hope that the fouled player will miss the foul shot. Mike Riordan began his successful NBA career with the Knicks as the designated fouler.

give up the body

vt: to place your body, while playing defense, in the path of an offensive player with the ball in an attempt to have a foul called on him.

glass

n: the backboard made out of plexiglass. Players use the glass to bank a shot into the basket; a bad shooter breaks the glass and a good rebounder goes to the glass.

goaltending

part: the act of inter~ fering with a shot when it is on a downward arc toward the basket, of blocking a shot after it has come off the back~ board on its way to the basket, or of interfering with a shot rolling on the rim of the basket. Each of these is a violation and results in 2 points against the offending team. It can be called *against* an offensive player, too, if he tips in a ball that is on the rim or in an imaginary cylinder extending up from the basket. In this case the goal is disallowed.

Patrick Ewing

go baseline

vt: to drive with the ball toward the basket along the end line.

go coast~ to~coast

vt: to take a rebound on the de~ fensive end, dribble the length of the floor, and score a basket, usually a layup or a dunk.

Magic Johnson is the best in the game at going coast~to~coast because he can combine his re~ bounding skill (he is 6~feet~9 inches tall), his dribbling skills, and his ability to find a path to the basket.

go to the boards

vt: to rebound missed shots, usually with an extra effort.

guard

vt: to play defense.
n: the position of a man playing the backcourt.

gunner

n: a player who at any time and from any place on the court is a threat to shoot. He is not necessarily always a threat to score.

Hail Mary

adj: the type of shot whose only chance to go in the basket is if the shot is accompanied by devout prayer.

half~court game

n: a patterned offensive style without much running: involves a lot of passing while the offense looks for a good shot.

hand check

vt: to place a hand lightly on the opposing player while playing defense.

hanger

n: a player who stays back near his own offensive basket hoping for a long pass and an easy shot while his teammates go down the floor on defense.

Tree Rollins

hatchet man

n: a player whose specialty is fouling, often with the purpose of taking the opposing team's star out of the game, either literally by causing a fight or an injury, or figuratively by making that player change his style of play in order to stay clear of the hatchet.

help

vt: to aid a teammate on defense.

high five

n: slapping palms with the arms extended above the shoulder.

high post

n: a spot on the floor near the foul circle where an offen~sive player, usually a center, will set up with his back to the basket and the offense will revolve around him.

George Mikan

hook shot

n: a high~arcing field~goal attempt made with your back to the basket with a high sweeping motion of the arm and a pivot of the foot opposite the shooting hand. Red Auerbach called George Mikan, who starred in the 1940s and 1950s, the greatest hook shooter in the history of the game.

hoop or hoops

n: the basket; or street slang for the game as in "Let's play some hoops."

horse

n (1): a variation on the game, usually played by two

(horse cont'd)

players and often on a basket tacked to a garage. Each player takes turns trying to make shots from different positions. His opponent has to duplicate any shot that goes in the basket. Everytime one player fails to make what his opponent already has made, he gets a letter — first an H, then an O, and so on, until one player spells the word HORSE, and loses.

(2): the player who does all the tough work, rebounding, playing defense against the opposition's top scorer, and scoring inside near the basket.

hurry-up offense

n: getting the ball down the floor as fast as possible, in a late-in-the-game attempt to cut an opposing team's lead.

Bob McAdoo

Ice

n: the coolest player on the court, one who is never fazed and never afraid to shoot. The San Antonio Spurs' George Gervin is the Iceman and has been so unafraid to shoot and is so good at it that he has led the NBA in scoring four times.

instant offense

n: what a player provides when coming off the bench; he immediately begins to shoot and score.

NEW INSTANT OFFENSE

in your face

prep. phrase: words uttered after one player has beaten another, either offensively with a move to the basket, or defensively with a particularly devastating block. The monologue usually goes like this, "In your face, sucker."

Alex English

J

n: a jump shot. The player who has a good one can "shoot the J."

jam

vt: to dunk the ball, as in "he jammed it in the basket;" or to block a shot, as in "he jammed it back in his face."

jump ball

n: the action that starts a game. Two opposing players stand in the circle at the center of the floor. The referee tosses the ball in the air and the play~ ers try to control the ball by tapping it to a teammate. A jump ball can also be called if two players simultaneously have control of the ball or if the refer~ ees' views are blocked as a ball goes out of bounds.

jump shot

n: a field goal attempt taken by leav~ ing your feet, jumping straight up in the

(jump shot cont'd)

air, and shooting the ball at the apex of your leap. When Hank Luisetti came to the East with his Stanford team in 1936, the shot had been used infre~ quently. But after Luisetti and Stan~ ford stunned and defeated a heavily~ favored Long Island University team, the shot became a big part of the game.

Hank Luisetti

Kangaroo

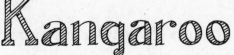

n: a player who jumps so well that some of his genes seem to come from this animal. When Billy Cunningham was a player at the University of North Carolina and later with the Philadelphia 76ers, he was known as the Kangaroo Kid.

Billy Cunningham

key

n: the area formed by the foul lane and the free~throw circle at the top of the lane. Origi~ nally called the Keyhole for that is its shape. A long shot is often taken from the top of the key.

kick it out

vi: to pass the ball out to a man away from the basket when play under the basket gets too crowded for a good shot.

Lane

n: two parallel lines extending from either end line that define an area behind which the players must stand when a free throw is being attempted.

layup

n: a shot taken directly in front of or just to the side of the basket. This shot is often banked off the backboard into the basket.

leather breath

n: what a player is said to have when his shot has been blocked right back in his face.

Ralph Sampson

lightbulb changer

n: a player who jumps so well it only takes one of him (and no ladder) to change a lightbulb.

loose~ball foul

n: a personal foul committed by a player who is trying to gain control of a ball when no one has possession of it.

lord of the rims

n: a player who is the dominating re~ bounder and one whom nobody will challenge in the area above the basket. This has been one of Kareem Abdul~ Jabbar's nicknames.

Lord Kareem I

losers

n: in a schoolyard game, the team that has given up the basket; in schoolyards generally, "losers out" means a team gets the ball after giving up a basket.

low post

n: a position near the basket taken by a player, usually with his back to the basket. Often the offense will revolve around a player in the low post if he is a particularly adept passer. Bill Walton and Wilt Chamber~ lain, in his later years, both excelled at this spot.

Man~to~man

n: a defense where each man takes one player on the opposing team and stays with him wherever he goes

(man~to~man)
on offense.

mental midget

n: a derogatory term for a player who makes dumb mistakes.

No harm, no foul

n: the loose style of play in which the officials call a foul only if a player seems to be hurt. As play gets looser, this term can escalate to no death, no foul, and finally no autopsy, no foul.

no~look pass

n: a pass thrown in one direction while looking in the other.

nose bleeder

n: a player who jumps so high he can suffer nose bleeds from the change in altitude.

Michael Cooper

Offensive boards

n: the backboard behind the basket you are shooting at.

offensive foul

n: a foul committed by a member of the offensive team that costs his team

possession of the ball, but does not result in free throws
for the fouled team.

open man

n: a player who is free to receive a pass and is in a good position to attempt a shot. Dave DeBusschere spent so many of his Knick seasons as the open man, that he used the term for the title of his autobiography.

Dave DeBusschere

outlaw school

n: a college that continually breaks NCAA rules to recruit players and then breaks some more to keep them eligible. In the 1970s Southwestern Louisiana broke more than one hundred rules and was forced to drop basketball for a few years.

outlet pass

n: a move that gets the ball quickly out from under one's defensive basket to a teammate heading downcourt. This pass often leads to a fast break. Wes Unseld of the Washington Bullets was the acknowledged master at this manuever and his skill at it resulted in his being named the NBA's most valuable player in his rookie season.

Wes Unseld

overtime

n: the extra period played after a game ends its regulation time with the teams tied.

Paint

n: the area in the foul lane that is a different color from the rest of the floor. A player who excels near the basket is "tough in the paint."

Jeff Ruland

palming

part: twisting the wrist while dribbling that results in the ball being carried; a violation that costs the team the ball.

pearl

n: any twisting offensive move that recall those of Earl (The Pearl) Monroe, who starred with the Baltimore Bullets and the New York Knicks.

Earl Monroe

peeker

n: a player, on defense, who tries to check the other offensive players by taking a peek at them while his man has the ball. Peekers who played against Elgin Baylor often were burned by him on baskets he made because of their mistakes.

penalty

n: what a team suffers when it exceeds its limit of personal fouls in a period. The penalty gives the fouled team an extra opportunity to sink a free throw on a foul committed in the act of shooting or two shots for what had previously been a non-shooting foul.

penetration

n: the act of getting inside an opposing team's defense, usually by dribbling and faking. Nate (Tiny) Archibald has long been acknowledged as one of the game's best at penetrating. He was so good, in fact, in the 1972-73 season that he led the NBA in scoring and assists.

Nate Archibald

perimeter shooter

n: a player who does most of his scoring from long range.

Brian Winters

personal foul

n: a violation committed when a player, either on offense or defense, has contact with an opponent.

Phi Slama Jama

n: a fraternity that came into existence in the 1982-83 season; the nickname of the University of Houston team that was runnerup for the

(Phi Slama Jama cont'd)

NCAA title in 1983. The name was derived from Houston's proclivity for dunk shots, a kind of Phi Beta Kappa of dunksmanship with Akeem Abdul Olajuwon and Clyde Drexler at the head of the class.

pick

n: the move when one offensive player stations himself in the line of a defensive player who is guarding the first man's teammate. This blocks the defensive player and allows the man he is defending against to get free.

pick and roll

n: a play where one player sets a pick and then moves to the basket, looking for a pass from the man whom he set the pick for.

pickup game

n: an unscheduled game, often played in the schoolyard, the gymnasiums of community centers, or YMCAs.

pill

n: the ball.

pin

vt: to stop the ball by holding it against the backboard; to pin the ball.

pivot

vi: to turn, often toward the basket, by keeping one

foot stationary and moving the other.

pivotman

n: the center, the player who stays nearest to the basket and around whom the offense revolves. The nature of the game has changed over the last several years so that one player doesn't stay planted near the basket. Henry (Dutch) Dehnert of the team called the Celtics in the 1920s (now known as the Original Celtics) is generally credited with inventing pivot play. The Celtics were the best team and often developed plays during a game with little fear of losing.

In one game Dehnert volunteered to stand with his back to the basket, receive a pass from his teammates and feed the ball back to them. But Dehnert discovered that if he pivoted away from his defensive man, he had a clear path to the basket. If defenses adjusted, he passed the ball to an open man.

Dutch Dehnert

player

n: a term of respect for someone who can play the game well and intelligently. There is no higher compliment than for one man to say of another, "He's a player."

point game

n: when one team needs just one basket to win a game that has a pre-arranged limit—in the schoolyard or YMCA it is often 21 baskets.

point guard

n: a backcourt man who is responsible for handling the ball and getting it to his teammates for shots. He directs and controls his team's offense.

Isiah Thomas

pop shot

n: a jump shot taken sud~denly, usually off the dribble.

post up

vt: to take advantage of a height mismatch or a mis~match created when a player has superior leaping ability in which one player brings the man guarding him near the basket to the low post, gets the ball and takes a shot over the defender. Reggie Theus of the Chicago Bulls frequently takes advan~tage of his 6~feet~6½ inches by posting up.

power forward

n: the frontcourt position often occupied by the team's strongest (though not necessarily tallest) player. He usually excels in re~bounding and defense.

Maurice Lucas

press

vt: to apply intense defensive pres~sure in an attempt to force the offensive team to lose the ball.

pump

vt: to bring the ball up toward the basket as if to shoot and then back down again before bringing it up for the actual shot.

push it up

vi: to get the ball upcourt quickly.

put the ball on the floor

vi: to dribble. Rarely does any~ one comment on the game and say a man dribbles; one now says he puts it on the floor. A player who is an adept drib~ bler "can put it on the floor." One who is not "shouldn't put it on the floor."

put toes in hoop

vi: to jump exceedingly well. Maurice Lucas of the Phoenix Suns says his young teammate Larry Nance "can put his toes in the hoop."

Rack

n: the rim. A player like Moses Malone spends much of his time going to the rack.

read a defense

Guy Rodgers

vi: to scan the oppo~ nents' defense and de~ termine what the defen~ sive players might do in a given situation. Ball~ handlers like Bob Cousy or Guy Rodgers were experts at reading defenses.

rebound

vt: to gain possession of a missed shot.

n: a missed shot that a player takes possession of.

red shirt

vt: to have a college player sit out a season, not because of injury, but to give him more time to mature and improve on his skills in practice without using up any eli~ gibility.

Buck Williams

rejection

n: the act of blocking a shot with some force and near the basket as if a wall had been erected to keep the ball away from the hoop.

reverse

n: a shot taken with the back to one side of the basket and with the ball going over the shooter's

head. This shot is often taken when a player is driv~
ing from the side toward the basket and a defender
can prevent a clear shot. The shooter keeps going,
past the rim and shoots the ball when he gets to
the other side of it.

rim

n: the metal ring that forms the basket.

ring~tailed howitzer

n: a line drive
shot that lands in
the basket area
with all the de~
structive force
of a big gun.

George Yardley

roads scholar

n: a college player who has been around; one who
spends some time at one school, finds things aren't
to his liking and then hits the road for another
school. Not to be confused with a Rhodes Scholar, an
award that can be earned for academic and athletic
achievement. Senator Bill Bradley of New Jersey and
Tom McMillen of the Atlanta Hawks are the two most
prominent of real Rhodes Scholars.

rock

n: the ball. To signify when a game is to start, you might say, "The rock goes in the air at 2."

roundball

n: a nickname, often derogatory, for the game of basketball. The late Red Smith, the Pulitzer Prize winning sports columnist, was never a fan of the game and never called it basketball, always roundball. "I never cared for back~and~forth sports," Red would say.

run and gun

vt: to keep up a fast pace in a game. To get the ball downcourt quickly and shoot at the first possible opportunity. In the pros, where a team has 24 seconds to shoot, a team that is running and gunning will rarely use more than 10 seconds of its allotted 24.

Russell elbows

n: what a player uses after he has grabbed a rebound and attempts to keep opponents from trying to take the ball away. First popularized by Bill Russell, the former great center of the Boston Celtics.

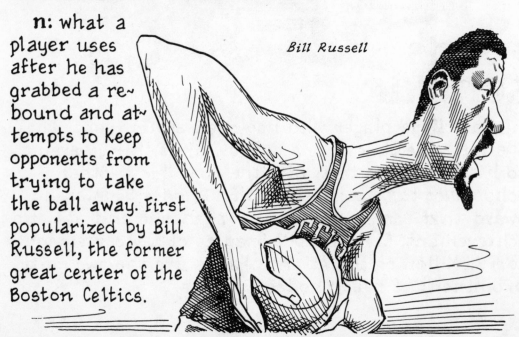

Bill Russell

Sag

vt: to let the man you are guarding go free while you help your teammate defend against another opposing player.

schoolyard

Connie Hawkins

n: where the game is played the most, on the courts in the play areas outside the schools. The rims are often bent, the nets are often missing, but virtually every player who has succeeded in the game began playing in the schoolyard. A player who excels in the schoolyard, but doesn't have the same flair when the games are more organized is called a schoolyard player. When a team in an organized game, in the NBA or in college for instance, gets into a helter-skelter style of play, they are said to be playing schoolyard ball. In New York, there are many schoolyard legends; one, Connie Hawkins had a successful NBA career after he had been barred by the NBA for several years for an alleged association with a gambler while he was a college freshman; two others, Earl (Goat) Manigault and Herman (Helicopter) Knowings, never were able to bring their skills to the public eye. Knowings, who was killed in a crash while

(schoolyard cont'd)

114 driving a taxi became so well known in New York, that his listing in the Bronx telephone book was Helicopter Knowings.

Larry Bird

scoop shot

n: an underhanded field goal attempt made while driving toward the basket with a motion that imitates someone scooping ice cream.

screen

n: the action of one offensive player moving in front of a defender to allow the teammate being guarded to get free for a shot or a drive to the basket.

Secretariat

n: a player who is a genuine thoroughbred, the best at his position, and one who dominates all other players at that position.

set shot

n: a two-hand shot taken with both feet firmly on the floor. Usually the shot is taken by grasping the ball with your hands on the sides or the back of it,

drawing the ball into your chest and moving the arms
back out, releasing the ball with the hands moving
toward the basket. This shot has lost its effectiveness,
because, though accurate, it is
easily blocked.

sewer

n: a basket in which every~
thing that comes near it goes
in.

Adrian
Dantley

shake
and bake

vt: to move toward the basket,
using every move and fake imaginable.

shirts   and skins

n: when two teams don't have
identifiable uniforms, one team
must keep its shirts on for the
game while the other must take
its shirts off and play bare~
chested. Typical of a school~
yard, a college intramural or
a community center game.

shooting
guard

n: the backcourt po~
sition player who is
the team's best shooter.

shot clock

n: the timing device that indicates how long a team has before it must shoot the ball; in the NBA there is a 24~second clock and a shot must either go in the basket or hit the rim or backboard in the allotted time. Otherwise the offensive team loses the ball. In some college conferences a shot clock has been introduced in recent years (some have 30 sec~ onds, some 45) in order to cut down on freezes, speed up the game, and increase the scoring.

sixth man

n: the first man to enter the game as a substitute. This non~starting position has been popularized over the years by the Boston Celtics whose coach, Red Auerbach, first used it with Frank Ramsey and then John Hav~ licek. Havlicek spent 16 years in the league and scored 26,395 points but for much of his career, he did not start a game. He was the most depend~ able Celtic and usually got as much playing time, if not more, than the players who did start. While he didn't start, he usually finished. As Auerbach often said, "don't ask me about the players who are in there at the

"Hondo"

beginning, ask me about the players who are in there 117
at the end."

skunk

vt: to shut out your opponents in a schoolyard game.

sky hook

World B. Free

n: a shot, taken beginning with your back toward the basket, then pivoting on one foot and shooting the ball with your hand and arm extended over your head. This shot was pop~ularized by Kareem Abdul~Jabbar and differs from the old~fashioned hook shot in that it is usually taken by players who are taller and the shot is released closer to the sky.

skywalker

n: a player who jumps so well he seems to walk on air.

slam dunk

n: what virtually all dunks are called nowadays. Usually done with a force that leaves the rim and backboard shaking. But in the cases of Gus Johnson of the old Baltimore Bullets and Darryl Dawkins of the New Jersey Nets, a slam dunk could break the rim and backboard.

small forward

n: the frontcourt position usually occupied by the team's best athlete. He is responsible for much of the shoot~ing and usually leads his team in scor~ing. He is often an adept passer and a non~stop runner. The player who makes his team move.

Bernard King, small forward

snatch

vt: to grab a rebound, usually off the fingertips of an opponent.

stall

vt: to hold the ball and try to use up time in an at~tempt to protect a lead or protect a player who is in foul trouble.

n: the style of play that enables a team to accom~plish this.

steal

vt: to take the ball away from an offensive player.

steps

n: the act of walking with the ball without dribbling it. When it is called, this violation costs a team pos~session of the ball.

strong side

n: the offensive area of the floor where most of the team with the ball is working it.

stuff

vt: to dunk the ball or to block a shot.

stunting

part: the tactic of a team shifting into varying defensive styles, usually from zone defense to man~to~man, as a means of confusing opponents.

stutter step

n: a herky~jerky move, a sort of hesitation step followed by a stride toward the basket designed to get the defensive player off balance.

submarine

vt: to get under a player after he has left his feet for a shot and then knock him off~balance. This is a dangerous manuever and often results in a fight.

suburban jump shot

n: a classic jump shot using per~fect form, usu~ally developed by players growing up in the suburbs of a big city, where the game is not so rough, and not in the inner~city school~yards, where most

of the scoring is done inside, near the basket. When Al McGuire was coaching at Marquette, he came to the Bronx to recruit Butch Lee of DeWitt Clinton High. Lee, McGuire said, "was an inner~city kid with a suburban jump shot."

SWISH!

n: the sound the net makes when your shot is so accurate that it does not hit the rim at all. Also the word used by many basketball an~ nouncers to describe such a shot.

Jerry West

switch

vt: to have two players on the same team change positions on defense, often after a teammate has been blocked out by an op~ posing player. When this happens, the player blocked out yells, "switch," and his teammate should understand that he must change men, even if he was not able to see all this action.

T n: the hand signal made by referees either to indicate a technical foul or that a team wants to take a timeout.

take it out

vt: to put the ball in play following a basket.

take it to the hoop

vt: to drive for a shot toward the basket.

technical foul

Kevin Loughery

n: a foul called when a coach or a player protests too long and/or loud to an official. The other team gets to shoot a free throw and also gets possession of the ball.

three

n: what the fans shout when a player has hit a long field goal that counts for three points, or when the player has made a basket and been fouled in the act of shooting. He is awarded a foul shot and an opportunity for a 3~point play.

three~D school

n: a college that recruits players but doesn't really prepare them for the future. A three~D school teaches no defense, no discipline, and offers no diploma.

three seconds

n: a violation called on an offensive player who stays in the foul lane more than three seconds. This rule was instituted to cut down on the dominance of the big men in the lane.

three~sixty

n: a showy dunk shot performed by spinning your body in a full circle as you go up toward the basket. This play has no other real purpose than to excite the crowd and, perhaps, embarass your opponent.

throw it down

vt: to dunk.

tickle the twine

vt: to hit nothing but the net on a shot. Used by some basketball announcers. to indicate such a shot.

tip in

vt: to tap a missed shot back through the hoop.

tomahawk dunk

n: a savage dunk shot, with the ball wedged in the crook of the elbow and with an arm action that loosely imitates the movement of hitting a block of wood with a tomahawk.

train

n: an unstoppable team, such as the Philadelphia

Darrell Griffith

76ers were in the 1983 playoffs.

transition game

n: the act of switching from offense to defense smoothly.

trap

n: a style of defense in which a player, as the second man chasing the player with the ball, puts himself in a position to prevent that man from moving with the ball or passing it.

traveling

part: taking too many steps with the ball without dribbling it. A violation.

triple double

n: the act of having 10 or more (known in basketball as double figures) points, rebounds, and assists in one game.

turkey

n: a player who is easily beaten.

Elgin Baylor, triple doubler

turnaround jumper

n: a shot taken by starting with the back to the basket, spinning toward the

(turnaround jumper cont'd.)

124 basket and leaping. The shot is taken facing the basket at the high point of the leap.

turnover

n: the act of giving the ball up on offense by either commit~ting a violation, a foul, losing the ball out of bounds, or having it stolen—without taking a shot at the basket.

Underhand free throw

n: a foul shot taken with the arms extended downward and both hands under or on the sides of the ball, then bringing the ball up and releasing it at around chest level towards the basket. Rick Barry was the last successful practitioner of this now almost lost art. Barry was so good at it, that he holds the career record in the NBA for free throw shooting.

Rick Barry

underneath

prep: the area below the basket where the big men dominate and the wise smaller men fear to tread.

up and down

vi: to jump, while holding the ball, and come down still holding it. A violation that costs the team the ball.

Violation

n: a transgression that costs the offensive team possession of the ball. Among violations are: traveling, three seconds, and palming.

Walking

part: carrying the ball without dribbling it or shooting it while taking steps. This is a violation.

weakside

n: the offensive side of the court away from the ball. When a backdoor play is executed properly, the man receiving the pass and taking the shot comes from the weakside.

weave

n: an offensive style in which all players on the offensive team keep moving around the ball and the ball is continually being passed. The aim is to get a man free underneath the basket by losing his opponent in the maze or by having him picked off during the movement.

wheel and deal

vi: to make all the tantalizing offensive moves (wheel) and then pass the ball off (deal).

Maurice Cheeks

Wilson sandwich

n: what a player eats—depending on the manufacturer of the ball being used—when he has a shot blocked back in his face. Another meal could be a Spalding sandwich.

wing

n: the position on either side of the offensive zone. Usually played by the team's best shooter, either a guard or a forward.

Yes

Marv Albert

inter: the sound uttered and made popular by Marv Albert with the Knicks championship teams to indicate that a shot was good.

Zebra

n: the referees; named for the striped shirts many of them wear.

zone defense

n: a style of defense, com~ mon in the college game but outlawed in the pros, in which each defensive player is responsible for an area of the floor, not for a particular offensive player. Although the zone defense is barred by the rules of professional basketball, every team in the NBA plays a zone of some kind at different points in a game. Among the best these days at using the zone with~ out detection are the Knicks and the 76ers.

zone trap

n: a variation on the zone defense in which the defenders try to force the ball into an area in which one of their players is there waiting to catch the man with the ball and steal it from him.

NICKNAMES

The nickname in basketball usually comes from the schoolyard or the park where the player first started. Tree Rollins lost his first name in a park in Cordele, Georgia. Julius Erving earned his degree in the playgrounds of Harlem. John Havlicek became Hondo at an Ohio high school all~star game. Others have acquired their nick~names because of their size (The Stilt, The Human Eraser, Truck) or their lack of it (Tiny). But for all, if people are talking basketball they know the nickname and how well they fit. Like, well, Magic.

Nate (Tiny) Archibald.

Archibald is called Tiny or sometimes Little Tiny, a double diminutive that aptly describes him but has nothing to do with his height. It has been estimated that he stands only 5~feet~10~inches although the NBA Register lists him at 6~feet~1 inch.

From the time Archibald was born on April 18, 1948, his given name of Nathaniel was almost nonexistent. On the South Bronx playgrounds, in the high school and college gymnasiums, and in the pros, he has always been Tiny Archibald.

"We always called him Tiny," said Julia Archibald, his mother. "The name had nothing to do with his size. He was rather a big baby, some eight pounds. We called his father Big Tiny, and him, Little Tiny."

Tiny, relatively speaking.

Wilt (The Stilt) Chamberlain

Wilt Chamberlain was 6~feet tall at age ten and 6~feet~3~ inches two years later when he graduated from grade school in Philadelphia. Halfway through Overbrook High School, Chamberlain was already 6~feet~11 inches. His street pals used to tease him about having to dip under door frames. Thus, his nickname, The Big Dipper, or to his friends sim~ ply, Dip, stemmed from the streets, though it was rein~ forced when he began to rise above baskets to dip basket~ balls through them. He always preferred Dip or Dipper to Wilt the Stilt, a name given him by Jack Ryan, a Philadel~ phia sports writer, and which Chamberlain felt made him seem like some monstrous, artificial man.

Julius (Dr. J.) Erving

The story goes that the first time Julius Erving showed up as a high school student to play in the Rucker summer tournament in New York, the public address an~ nouncer found himself searching for ways to describe the previously unheard of performer. He began by affix~ ing all of the most banal nicknames on Julius. He used names like The Claw, Black Moses, Magic, and Little Hawk. But during one of the timeouts, Julius walked over to him and said, "Just call me The Doctor." He did, and the name stuck.

Walt (Clyde) Frazier

Clyde, minus Bonnie

The name of the book Walt Frazier wrote with Joe Jares was entitled, *Clyde*. The title of chapter one is "Nobody Calls Me Walt Anymore." Although much of the credit was given Danny Whalen, the Knick trainer, for the Clyde moniker, Frazier credits Nate Bowman,

then the Knicks' substitute center. When Frazier came to the 131
Knicks, it was just after the release of the movie about
the Depression~era gangsters, *Bonnie and Clyde*. Warren
Beatty, playing the role of Clyde Barrow, favored wide~
brim fedora hats as did Frazier. On a road trip, Frazier
bought a cocoa~brown wide~brim hat made of Italian
velour. The first time Bowman laid eyes on it, he coined
the nickname. Because Frazier made a good deal of his
star's reputation as a pro by
stealing—stealing the ball
from opponents—the nickname
was reinforced.

World B. Free

World B. Free

Most nicknames are given
to one person by another. Some
stick all through life, but few if
any ever become a legal name.
At Howard Park, the Brownsville
Recreation Center, P.S. 32 and 66
schoolyards, all in the Brownsville
section of Brooklyn, Lloyd Free was
All~World. He said so himself. He got
that name as a fourteen~year old and he kept it
through his high school, college, and early pro days. In
1982, the springy 6~feet~2~inch guard, changed his
name legally from Lloyd B. Free to World B. Free.

George (The Iceman) Gervin

In Gervin's first pro season with the Virginia Squires
of the American Basketball Association, he was not a
big star, but did manage to average 14 points a game
and make the league's all~rookie team. He played on
that Virginia team alongside Julius Erving and Fatty

(George Gervin cont'd)

132

Taylor, who tagged Gervin, the Iceman. Taylor christened Gervin in tribute to his cool demeanor on the court. Gervin has lived up to the name ever since. On the court, he never hurries. He always seems to run at half speed, taking the easy way. He seldom plays up to the fans, rarely exerting himself to make a startling dunk shot when he is wide open. Instead, he just lays the ball in slowly. It's worth the same 2 points.

John (**Hondo**) Havlicek

Hondo

Havlicek grew up in eastern Ohio. He was born in Martins Ferry, lived in Lansing, attended Bridgeport High School and received his mail in Adenna. He hung around the family store in Dillonville. The first time he got a real glimpse of the outside world was when he went to play in a high school All-Star game. "I met Jerry Lucas and Larry Siegfried at the game," Havlicek recalled naming two of the Ohio stars of that era who became Havlicek's teammates at Ohio State. "We became good friends. One night five of us, including Mel Nowell went to see John Wayne in the movie, *Hondo*. Mel couldn't pronounce my last name, and he said I looked like John Wayne from the side. That was the way the nickname Hondo was born."

Earvin (**Magic**) Johnson

Fred Stabley Jr., a sports writer for *The Lansing (Michigan) Journal*, is responsible for the nickname, of Magic. He gave him the name after Johnson, playing for Everett

(Earvin Johnson cont'd.)

High School had scored 36 points, grabbed 18 rebounds, and had 16 assists in a game. After the game, Stabley approached Johnson and said, "I've got to give you a nickname. I can't call you Dr. J because that is already taken and I can't call you Big E because that belongs to Elvin Hayes." The performance, Stabley decided, was magical, and the name appeared in the headlines of the next day's newspaper.

Jim (**Jungle Jim**) Loscutoff

The late Howie McHugh, the long-time publicity director of the Boston Celtics, would tell the story of the night a group of fans actually invaded the Celtic huddle. "Jungle Jim and Gene Conley were knocking them down as fast as they came," McHugh said. "Then a cop lost his hat and Jim belted him by mistake." Jim Loscutoff toiled in the NBA with the Celtics for eight seasons as a good rebounder who spent much of his time setting im~ movable picks. He was 6~ feet~6 inches, 230 pounds. He was built wide and had a mean look, thus the name, Jungle Jim. Red Auerbach, who was coaching the Celtics at the time, called him "my friendly bruiser."

Maurice (**The Enforcer**) Lucas

The 6~feet~9~inch Lucas never planned it that way, but he gained a quick reputation as "the enforcer" when

134 he began his pro career in 1974 with the Spirits of St. Louis in the ABA. Lucas decked 7~foot~2~inch Artis Gilmore, then of the Kentucky Colonels, during an oncourt struggle. His reputation as an intimidator grew when he played with the Portland Trail Blazers and was looked upon as Bill Walton's guardian. He kept the NBA muscle men off the fragile Walton. During the 1977 playoffs Lucas fought Darryl Dawkins, the 6~feet~11 inch, 250~pound Philadelphia 76ers' center, in the championship round. Even if Lucas had not been noted for his rough play, Al McGuire, Lucas's coach at Marquette, points out, "It's because of Luke's body that the title of enforcer is there."

Cornbread

Cedric Maxwell (Cornbread)

Cedric Maxwell, with his rubber~band body that inspired more chuckles than awe, and the University of North Carolina at Charlotte, were unheralded when they arrived for the 1977 National Invitation Tournament at Madison Square Garden. But as the tourney progressed, fans were seen running round the Garden in Cornbread t~shirts. That was the kind of effect Maxwell, a junior at the time, had on the crowd as he walked away with the most valuable player honors. The nickname came in college because of his resemblance in looks and playing style to Jamaal Wilkes, the Los Angeles Lakers' forward, who was starring at the time in a movie called Cornbread, Earl and Me.

(Cedric Maxwell cont'd)

Maxwell doesn't like the nickname and prefers to be called Max.

Dick (Tricky Dick) McGuire

Dick McGuire, the Knicks' top draft choice in 1949, played in the rugged era of NBA development. Together with Bob Cousy, he seemingly invented passes that flashed through herds of big men to driving guards and forwards. Although not equal to Cousy offensively, McGuire was considered one of the game's greatest playmakers and passers. His court smarts, slick passing, and ball handling earned him the nickname of Tricky Dick.

Tricky Dick

Earl (The Pearl) Monroe

It fits. The nickname has just the correct show business ring because on the basketball court Earl Monroe was the consumate showman. His style was all his own as he weaved, wiggled his hips, and slid his feet. The Monroe legend grew while he was attending Winston~Salem College, a predominantly black school in the heart of North Carolina tobacco country. The sports information director gave Monroe the nickname of Pearl for his jewel~like moves and the smooth sound the name had. When Monroe would take his man into the corner, spin, and hit the jumper, the crowd would respond with "Earl, Earl, Earl the Pearl." The chant followed him throughout his NBA career. Monroe helped the Pearl legend grow. Soon, he began to wear a gold necklace that read, "Pearl." From the "A" a black pearl was suspended. In the mid~70s a woman named Pearl Moore was one of the top college players in the nation. She had all the moves and so, naturally, she was called Pearl (The Earl) Moore.

Richard (Digger) Phelps

Phelps, the Notre Dame coach, is the son of an undertaker from Beacon, New York. A friend in seventh grade gave the younger Phelps the name, based on his father's profession.

Oscar (The Big O) Robertson

When Eddie Donovan was the Knick coach, he came upon a unique way to describe the talents of Oscar Robertson, considered the most complete and effective player in the history of the game. "The man has everything," Donovan said. "He could easily be a sculptor's answer if he was commandeered to lump into one form the elements that made the perfect player." Throughout college and his 13-season pro career, he was The Big O, a nickname that made it easy for headline writers and layout men to exploit the scoring, rebounding, and passing feats of the 6-foot-5-inch guard. Hardly a day passed without some publication having a photograph of a big O, with Robertson's picture set in the center.

Leonard (Truck) Robinson

On Len Robinson's white sneakers is the word: T-R-U-C-K. Then there is the matter of a poster — Robinson clad in a red flannel shirt, jeans, bright red suspenders, and baseball cap. The Knick power forward, portraying the true, gritty, blue collar worker, is sitting on the front fender of an 18-wheeler. At the bottom of the poster there's that word again, T-R-U-C-K. To the world, trucks are big and they are built to pull and

get things done. That has been the way the 6~foot~7~inch,
235~pound Robinson has operated since he came into the
NBA as the 1974 second~round draft choice of the Washing~
ton Bullets.

Wayne (Tree) Rollins

During his days growing up in Cordele, Georgia, Rollins
has recalled, there was a park where he played most of
his basketball. "Go to any park where black kids are play~
ing," Rollins says. "Then just listen for 15 minutes. Every
kid has a nickname. We had a T~Man, Tank~Head, Zay, Iron
Head, and No Neck. Mine was Tree." (Of course, Wayne Rollins
was the tallest kid in the park.) "Oliske Putnam, who worked
at a gas station and whose nickname was BoTab, just
started calling me Tree and it stuck."

Adolph (The Baron) Rupp

In the Commonwealth of Kentucky
a governor cannot succeed himself
and a horse can run only once in
the Derby, but in Bluegrass Coun~
try, Adolph Rupp, the Univer~
sity of Kentucky basketball
coach, was always there. His
teams won 879 games during 42
years as the Wildcat coach and
Rupp was often referred to as
"The Baron" or "The Man in the
Brown Suit." He had a 500~acre estate in the pleasant,

The Baron

rolling countryside outside Lexington where he tended
to his prize Herefords and grew Burley tobacco. For this
he was often called the "Baron of Bluegrass Country." His name
as "The Man in the Brown Suit" stemmed from his supersti~
tious preference for brown as the color of his game~night
wardrobe.

Marvin (The Human Eraser) Webster

Marvin Webster, the only 7-footer on the block when he was a high school student in West Baltimore, was then called Marvin the Magnificent. After he started averaging 20 rebounds a game and after becoming a ferocious shot blocker in college at Morgan State, Marvin the Magnificent became the Human Eraser.

Charles (Buck) Williams

As a boy growing up in Rocky Mount, North Carolina, Williams was so stocky that a friend of the family began calling him Huckabuck, which, in the argot of the eastern part of North Carolina, means a large hulking person. Huckabuck was eventually shortened to Buck.

John (The Wizard) Wooden

Dwight Chapin and Jeff Prugh collaborated to write a book entitled, *The Wizard of Westwood*, their biography of John Wooden, the UCLA basketball coach. The Wizard of Westwood is how they refer to Wooden on the Westwood campus of UCLA for his wizardry in developing the greatest college basketball power ever—one that won ten NCAA championships in twelve seasons.

INDEX

ABC, 66

ABC Sports, 66

Abdul-Jabbar, Kareem, 16, 25, 28, 32, 33–36, 38, 57, 60, 75, 101, 117

Air ball, 75

Aircraft carrier, 75

Albert, Marv, 126

Alcindor, Lew, 25, 38

Alley oop, 75

American Basketball Association, 15, 26, 30, 58, 66, 76, 131

Anderson, Dave, 46

Archibald, Nate, 105, 129

Arledge, Roone, 66

Assist, 76

Atlanta Hawks, 21, 66, 68, 111

Auerbach, Red, 14, 17, 21–24, 41, 42, 46, 53, 85, 96, 116, 133

Axthelm, Pete, 18, 81

Backcourt, 76

Backdoor, 77

Baechtold, Jim, 69

Baltimore Bullets, 104, 117

Bank shot, 77

Barnett, Dick, 53, 88

Barry, Rick, 30, 124

Baseball pass, 77

Baseline, 78

Basketball Association of America, 37

Basketball Hall of Fame, 24, 38, 42

Baylor, Elgin, 54, 104, 123

Beatty, Warren, 131

Belly up, 78

Belmont Abby College, 49, 50

Bird, Larry, 114

Blue Demons, 50

Boards, 78

Bonnie and Clyde, 54, 131

Bonus, 78

Boryla, Vince, 69

Boston Celtics, 14, 15, 16, 21, 22, 24, 34, 41–42, 45–46, 53, 68, 112, 116, 133

Boston Garden, 14, 15, 21, 24, 42, 45

Bowling Green, 46

Bowman, Nate, 130

Box out, 78

Bradley, Bill, 17, 53, 77, 111

Braun, Carl, 69

Braves, Buffalo, 29

Break the ice, 79

Brick, 79

Broadwood Hotel, 37

Brooklyn Visitations, 70

Brown, Freddy, 86

Bucket, 79

Bucks, Milwaukee, 29, 33, 34, 36, 66, 75

Buffalo Braves, 29

Bullets, Baltimore, 104, 117

Bullets, Washington, 103, 137

Bulls, Chicago, 108

Burn, 79

Buss, Jerry, 60

Buzzer, 80

Calverley, Ernie, 14

Candy Slam, 64

Capitals, Washington, 21

Carolina Cougars, 66

Carter, Fred, 21

Cavaliers, Cleveland, 56

Celtics, Boston, 14, 15, 16, 21, 22, 24, 34, 41–42, 45–46, 53, 68, 112, 116, 133

Celtics, Original, 37, 41, 70, 107

Center, 80

Chamberlain, Wilt, 14, 16, 17, 25, 33, 38, 42, 44, 54, 64, 80, 87, 101, 130

Chaminade of Hawaii, 84

Charging, 80

Cheeks, Maurice, 28, 126

Chicago Bulls, 108

Chicago Stags, 46, 48

Chippie, 81

Chones, Jim, 50

Chopper, 81

Chump, 81

City College (New York), 70

City game, 81

City Game, The, 18

Clancy, Michael, 30

Cleveland Cavaliers, 56

Clippers, San Diego, 57

Clutch, 82

Colonels, Kentucky, 134

Conley, Gene, 133

Connery, Sean, 33

Conquistadors, San Diego, 15

Cool, 82

Cooper, Michael, 102

Cornbread, Earl and Me, 134

Cougars, Carolina, 66

Court smarts, 82

Cousy, Bob, 42, 45–48, 110, 135

Cowens, Dave, 77

Cross-court pass, 83

Cunningham, Billy, 16, 62, 99

Curtain time, 83

D, 83

Dance, 83

140

Dance-hall player, 84
Dantley, Adrian, 115
Dartmouth College, 49
Dawkins, Darryl, 61–64, 81, 117, 134
Deal, 84
DeBusschere, Dave, 32, 44, 53, 56, 77, 166
Dee-fense, 84
Dehnert, Henry, 107
Denver Nuggets, 30, 76
De Paul University, 50
Derek, Bo, 52
DeWitt Clinton High School, 120
Dish, 85
Doctor, 85
Donovan, Eddie, 136
Double dribble, 85
Double figures, 85
Double pump, 86
Double team, 86
Downtown, 86
Drexler, Clyde, 106
Dunk, 87

East Cupcake, 87
Embry, Wayne, 34
Eraser, 87
Erving, Julius, 15, 16, 25–28, 62, 130, 131
Ewing, Patrick, 93

Facial, 88
Fadeaway jumper, 88
Fall back, 88
Fast break, 88
Filling the lanes, 88
Finger roll, 89
Fire the rock, 89
Fitch, Gil, 37
Flow, 89
Foul shot, 90
Four corners, 90
Frazier, Walt, 53–56, 130
Free, Lloyd B., 131
Free, World B., 117, 131
Free foul, 90

Freeze, 91
French pastry, 91
Fulks, Joe, 38
Fullcourt press, 91

Gallatin, Harry, 69
Garbage man, 91
Garbage time, 92
Garden, Boston, 14, 15, 21, 24, 42, 45
Garden, Madison Square, 13, 17, 53, 54, 56, 70, 72, 84, 134
Gervin, George, 89, 97, 131
Get back, 92
Gilmore, Artis, 134
Give and go, 92
Give one, 92
Give up the body, 93
Glass, 93
Globetrotters, Harlem, 17
Goaltending, 93
Go baseline, 93
Go coast-to-coast, 94
Golden State Warriors, 34
Go to the boards, 94
Gottlieb, Eddie, 37–40, 48
Grunfeld, Ernie, 50
Guard, 94
Guerin, Richie, 66
Gunner, 94

Hagerty, Horse, 70
Hail Mary, 14, 95
Half-court game, 95
Hall of Fame, Basketball, 24, 38, 42
Hand check, 95
Hanger, 95
Hanzlik, Bill, 30
Harlem Globetrotters, 17
Harlem Professional League, 25
Harris, Bucky, 13
Hatchet man, 49, 95
Havlicek, John, 116, 132
Hawkins, Connie, 25, 113
Hawks, Atlanta, 21, 66, 68, 111
Hawks, Tri-City, 46

Hayes, Elvin, 32, 58
Heinsohn, Tom, 15, 22
Help, 96
High five, 96
High post, 96
Holiday Festival, 72
Holman, Nat, 70
Holy Cross College, 45, 46
Holyoke Reds, 70
Holzman, Red, 84
Hook shot, 96
Hoop(s), 96
Horse, 96
Hosket, Bill, 53
Houston, University of, 105
Houston Rockets, 29, 30, 32
Hudson, Lou, 68
Human Eraser, 87
Hurry-up offense, 97

Ice, 97
Iceman, 89, 97
Instant offense, 97
In your face, 98
Irish, Ned, 48

J, 98
Jam, 98
Jazz, New Orleans, 66, 68
Jazz, Utah, 68
Jewels, New York, 37
Johnson, Earvin, 28, 57–30, 132
Johnson, Gus, 117
Jump ball, 98
Jump shot, 98

Kangaroo, 99
Kansas City Kings, 62
Kaselman, Cy, 37
Kentucky, University of, 49, 137
Kentucky Colonels, 134
Key, 99
Kick it out, 99
King, Bernard, 118
Kings, Kansas City, 62

Knicks, New York, 14, 16, 17, 30, 44, 48, 53, 54, 56, 69, 70, 77, 81, 82, 92, 103, 104, 126, 127, 130, 136
Knowings, Herman, 113

Lakers, Los Angeles, 16, 17, 22, 28, 30, 32, 33, 54, 57, 58, 60, 75, 82, 134
Lane, 100
Lanier, Bob, 29
Lapchick, Joe, 16, 69–72
Layup, 100
Leather breath, 100
Lee, Butch, 120
Lightbulb changer, 100
Long Island University, 13, 99
Loose-ball foul, 101
Lord of the rims, 101
Los Angeles Lakers, 16, 17, 22, 28, 30, 32, 33, 54, 57, 58, 60, 75, 82, 134
Loscutoff, Jim, 133
Losers, 101
Loughery, Kevin, 121
Louisiana State, 65
Low post, 101
Loyola of Chicago, 46
Lucas, Jerry, 132
Lucas, Maurice, 108, 109, 133
Luisetti, Hank, 13, 41, 99

McAdoo, Bob, 58
McGlocklin, Jon, 34
McGuire, Al, 49–52, 69, 87, 120, 134
McGuire, Dick, 135
McHugh, Howie, 133
McKeithen, John, 65
McKinney, Jack, 58
McMahon, Jack, 64
McMillen, Tom, 111
Madison Square Garden, 13, 17, 53, 54, 56, 70, 72, 84, 134
Malone, Moses, 16, 28, 29–32, 64, 79, 109
Manigault, Earl, 113

Man-to-man, 101
Maravich, Pete, 65–68
Maravich, Press, 65
Marquette University, 50, 52, 120, 134
Massachusetts, University of, 26
Maxwell, Cedric, 134
Meekan, Stretch, 37
Meminger, Dean, 50, 52
Mental midget, 102
Meyers, Ray, 52
Michigan, University of, 72
Michigan State, 57, 58
Mikan, George, 36, 96
Mikkelsen, Vern, 84
Milwaukee Bucks, 29, 33, 34, 36, 66, 75
Mississippi State, 66
Monroe, Earl, 53, 104, 135
Moore, Pearl, 135
Morgan State, 138

Naismith, James, 11, 12
Nance, Larry, 109
NBA, 15, 16, 21, 33, 38, 42, 44, 45, 50, 53, 54, 58, 60, 61, 64, 65, 66, 70, 82, 91, 92, 103, 105, 113, 116, 124, 127, 133, 135
NBC, 52
NCAA, 33, 41, 49, 52, 58, 83, 103, 106, 138
Nets, New Jersey, 64, 117
Nets, New York, 15
Newell, Pete, 34
New Jersey Nets, 64, 117
New Orleans Jazz, 66, 68
New York Jewels, 37
New York Knicks, 14, 16, 17, 30, 44, 48, 53, 54, 56, 69, 70, 77, 81, 82, 92, 103, 104, 126, 127, 130, 136
New York Nets, 15
Nissalke, Tom, 30
NIT, 14, 54, 69, 72, 134
Nixon, Norm, 82
No harm, no foul, 102
No-look pass, 102

North Carolina, University of, 134
North Carolina State, 76
Nose bleeder, 52, 102
Notre Dame, 136
Nuggets, Denver, 30, 76

O'Brien, Larry, 64
Offensive boards, 102
Offensive foul, 102
Ohio State, 132
Olajuwon, Akeem Abdul, 106
Open man, 103
Original Celtics, 37, 41, 70, 107
Outlaw school, 103
Outlet pass, 103
Overtime, 104

Paint, 104
Palming, 104
Park, Howard, 131
Passon, Chickie, 37
Pearl, 104
Peeker, 104
Penalty, 105
Penetration, 105
Perimeter shooter, 105
Personal foul, 105
Phelps, Richard, 136
Philadelphia 76ers, 16, 29, 30, 60, 61, 62, 64, 122, 127, 134
Philadelphia Warriors, 14, 38, 42, 48
Phillips, Andy, 48
Phi Slama Jama, 105
Phoenix Suns, 15, 21
Pick, 106
Pick and roll, 106
Pickup game, 106
Pill, 106
Pin, 106
Pivot, 106
Pivotman, 107
Player, 107
Point game, 107
Point guard, 108
Pop shot, 108
Porter, Kevin, 91

142

Portland Trail Blazers, 89, 134
Post up, 108
Power forward, 108
Power Memorial Academy, 33, 38
Press, 108
Professional Basketball Writers
  Association, 33
Pump, 109
Push it up, 109
Put the ball on the floor, 109
Put toes in hoop, 109

Rack, 109
Ramsey, Frank, 116
Read a defense, 110
Rebound, 110
Reds, Holyoke, 70
Red shirt, 110
Reed, Willis, 16, 17, 25, 32, 34,
  53, 56
Rejection, 110
Reverse, 110
Rhode Island College, 14
Rhodes Scholars, 111
Rim, 111
Ring-tailed howitzer, 111
Riordan, Mike, 92
Roads scholar, 111
Robertson, Oscar, 68, 90, 91, 136
Robinson, Leonard, 136
Robinson, Oscar, 65
Robinzine, Bill, 67
Rock, 112
Rockets, Houston, 29, 30
Rockets, San Diego, 58
Rodgers, Guy, 110
Rollins, Wayne, 95, 137
Roundball, 112
Rucker Memorial Playground, 25,
  130
Run and gun, 112
Rupps, Adolph, 49, 137
Russell, Bill, 14, 15, 16, 21, 22,
  33, 34, 36, 41–44, 85, 112
Russell, Cazzie, 17
Russell elbows, 112
Ryan, Jack, 130

Sag, 113
St. John's University, 69, 70, 72
St. John's Wonder Five, 37
Sampson, Ralph, 84, 100
San Antonio Spurs, 62, 97
San Diego Clippers, 57
San Diego Conquistadors, 15
San Diego Rockets, 58
San Francisco, University of, 21,
  34, 41
Schaus, Fred, 69
Schoolyard, 113
Scoop shot, 114
Screen, 114
Seattle SuperSonics, 42, 86
Secretariat, 114
Senators, Washington, 13
Set shot, 114
76ers, Philadelphia, 16, 29, 30, 60,
  61, 62, 64, 122, 127, 134
Sewer, 115
Shake and bake, 115
Share, Charley, 46
Shirts and skins, 115
Shooting guard, 115
Shot clock, 116
Siegfried, Larry, 132
Silas, Paul, 78, 79
Sixth man, 116
Skunk, 117
Skyhook, 57, 117
Skywalker, 117
Slam dunk, 117
Small forward, 118
Smith, Dean, 90
Smith, Red, 112
Snatch, 118
Southern Illinois, 54
Southern Philadelphia Hebrew
  Association, 37
Southwestern Louisiana, 103
Spalding sandwich, 126
Spectrum, 62
Spirits of St. Louis, 134
Spurs, San Antonio, 62, 97
Squires, Virginia, 26, 131
Stags, Chicago, 46, 48
Stall, 118
Stanford University, 13, 41, 99

Stars, Utah, 30
Steal, 118
Steps, 118
Strong side, 118
Stuff, 119
Stunting, 119
Stutter step, 119
Submarine, 119
Suburban jump shot, 119
Suns, Phoenix, 15, 21
SuperSonics, Seattle, 42, 86
Swish, 120
Switch, 120

T, 120
Take it out, 120
Take it to the hoop, 121
Taylor, Fatty, 131
Technical foul, 121
Temple University, 28
Theus, Reggie, 108
Thomas, Isiah, 108
Thompson, David, 76
Three, 121
Three-D school, 121
Three seconds, 121
Three-sixty, 122
Throw it down, 122
Tickle the twine, 122
Tip in, 122
Tomahawk dunk, 122
Towe, Monte, 76
Trail Blazers, Portland, 89, 134
Train, 122
Transition game, 123
Trap, 123
Traveling, 123
Tri-City Hawks, 46
Triple double, 123
Tripucka, Kelly, 91
Turkey, 123
Turnaround jumper, 123
Turnover, 124

UCLA, 33, 49, 75, 138
Underhand free throw, 124
Underneath, 124

Unseld, Wes, 103
Up and down, 125
Utah Jazz, 68
Utah Stars, 30

Van Breda Kolff, Butch, 69
Villanova University, 72
Violation, 125
Virginia Squires, 26, 131
Visitation Hall, 37
Visitations, Brooklyn, 70

Walker, Chet, 89
Walking, 125
Walton, Bill, 89, 101, 134

Warriors, Golden State, 34
Warriors, Philadelphia, 14, 38, 42, 48
Washington Bullets, 103, 137
Washington Capitals, 21
Washington Senators, 13
Wayne, John, 132
Weakside, 125
Weave, 125
Webster, Marvin, 87, 138
West, Jerry, 54, 58, 68, 82, 120
Westhead, Paul, 36
Whalen, Danny, 130
Wheel and deal, 126
Wilkes, Jamaal, 134
Williams, Buck, 110
Williams, Charles, 138

Wilson sandwich, 126
Wing, 126
Winston-Salem College, 135
Winters, Brian, 105
Wizard of Westwood, The, 138
Wooden, John, 49, 138

Yardley, George, 111
Yes, 126
YMCA, 11, 12

Zaslofsky, Max, 48
Zebra, 127
Zone defense, 127
Zone trap, 127